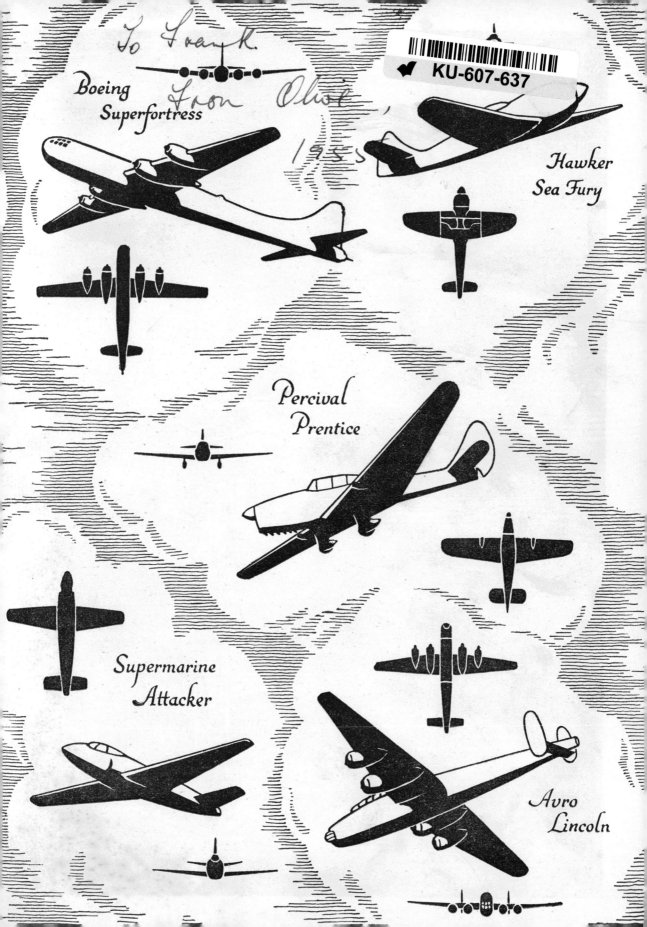

Boeing
Superfortress

Hawker
Sea Fury

Percival
Prentice

Supermarine
Attacker

Avro
Lincoln

THE WONDER BOOK

OF THE

R.A.F.

A METEOR PILOT AND HIS FLYING GEAR.

VICKERS SUPERMARINE "SWIFT"

THE WONDER BOOK

OF THE

R.A.F.

*WITH EIGHT COLOUR PLATES
AND OVER 200 ILLUSTRATIONS*

Fifth Edition

WARD, LOCK & CO., LIMITED
LONDON AND MELBOURNE

THE WONDER BOOK SERIES

EACH WITH 8 COLOUR PLATES AND
HUNDREDS OF ILLUSTRATIONS

THE WONDER BOOK OF BIBLE STORIES
Stories from the Old and New Testaments that live for ever, retold in an easily understandable way for children.

THE WONDER BOOK OF THE FARM
Describes all aspects of modern farming and its place in our day-to-day life.

THE WONDER BOOK OF THE R.A.F.
All about our glorious Air Force.

THE WONDER BOOK OF AIRCRAFT
Illustrating and describing all the wonderful developments in civil aviation.

THE WONDER BOOK OF ANIMALS
This very popular volume is not merely a picture book, or a story book, or a natural history book, but a blend of all three, with many entertaining and instructive features.

THE WONDER BOOK OF RAILWAYS
Scores of chatty articles about railways and locomotives all over the world.

THE WONDER BOOK OF SHIPS
All about the great liners and other ships of the Merchant Navy.

THE WONDER BOOK OF THE ARMY
Romance and adventure of the modern soldier.

THE WONDER BOOK OF THE NAVY
All about the Navy of to-day.

THE WONDER BOOK OF WHY & WHAT ?
Answers to children's questions on all sorts of subjects, with hundreds of pictures.

THE WONDER BOOK OF WONDERS
The most wonderful things in the world fascinatingly described and illustrated.

THE WONDER BOOK OF NATURE
Every child is at heart a lover of Nature and the open air. Boys and girls of all ages will be delighted with this volume.

THE WONDER BOOK OF MOTORS
Aptly described as " the Rolls-Royce " of gift books.

THE WONDER BOOK OF SCIENCE
Some of the most famous authorities tell the story of modern discoveries and theories.

THE WONDER BOOK OF DO YOU KNOW ?
Tells in picture and story of some of the most wonderful things in the world—many of them in our own homes.

THE WONDER BOOK OF TELL ME WHY ?
Answers to numbers of those puzzling questions that begin with the words How ? When ? Why ? and What ?

THE WONDER BOOK OF HOW IT'S DONE
A brightly written and lavishly illustrated volume describing numbers of the interesting things a child sees in the course of a day, telling how they work, or how they are made.

THE WONDER BOOK OF WOULD YOU BELIEVE IT ?
Many strange and wonderful things that are nevertheless true are described and illustrated in this fascinating volume.

THE WONDER BOOK OF THINGS TO DO
Provides not one solution, but many, to the perpetual question, " What can I do ? "

THE STORY WONDER BOOK
Delightful pictures and stories for boys and girls of all ages.

MADE IN ENGLAND
Printed in Great Britain by Butler & Tanner Ltd., Frome and London

[*By courtesy of the Hawker Siddeley Group.*

HAWKER " HUNTER " AVRO-ENGINED JET FIGHTER IN WHICH SQUADRON-LEADER NEVILLE
DUKE RECAPTURED THE WORLD'S SPEED RECORD FOR GREAT BRITAIN WITH AN AVERAGE
SPEED OF 727 M.P.H. (September 7th, 1953). See also illustration, page 19.

COLOUR PLATES

GLOSTER JAVELIN, DELTA-WINGED, TWIN-JET, MULTI-PURPOSE FIGHTER.

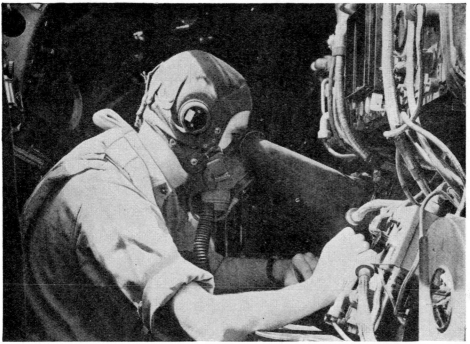

[Crown Copyright.

THE NAVIGATOR OF A BOMBER CHECKS HIS POSITION BY RADAR.

CONTENTS

THE HANDLEY PAGE "VICTOR" FOUR-JET BOMBER.
Showing the large air-intakes and engine housing in the wing roots.

["*Flight*" *Photos.*

THE SHORT BROTHERS AND HARLAND S.B.5.
An experimental jet plane for research into the problems of wing sweep-back. Like the Javelin and Victor it has a high-mounted tailplane.

THE PERCIVAL PROVOST WITH ALVIS LEONIDES ENGINE.

FOREWORD

By Air Vice-Marshal Sir Charles Longcroft,
K.C.B., C.M.G., D.S.O., A.F.C.

WHEN a young man joins the Royal Air Force he discovers that he shares a record of achievement and a tradition that cannot be matched by any other air force in the world; a legacy made up of great triumphs, of gallantry and noble deeds which mould the conduct and shape the character of all who wear the uniform of England's youngest fighting Service.

This book tells about some of the past glories of the Royal Air Force, and of the two Services out of which it grew—the Royal Flying Corps and the Royal Naval Air Service. But, chiefly, it is concerned with the Royal Air Force of to-day—with jet bombers and jet fighters, radar and a score of other devices which were quite unknown when, in 1912, the Royal Flying Corps was formed and a handful of Naval and Army officers volunteered to learn the uncertain business of piloting aeroplanes and putting them to military use.

FOREWORD

Some of those officers have seen the whole pattern of military aeronautics unfold, and as one of them I never cease to wonder at the great change which the aeroplane brought about in naval and military affairs. It may be your lot to see still greater changes.

[*Keystone.*

JET-AGE CADETS AT CRANWELL STUDY A GLOBE OF THE WORLD.

[De Havilland Photo.

THE D.H.110, TWIN-ENGINE TURBO-JET DAY AND NIGHT FIGHTER.
The first British two-seater aircraft to exceed the speed of sound. It is being developed as a Naval aircraft.

THE GLORIOUS TRADITION
OF THE R.A.F.

FEW suspected, when the flying age dawned, that Great Britain could ever become great in the air. The world was ruled, then, by Sea Power, and for centuries England had held undisputed command of the seas. The aeroplane seemed to offer a threat to the sovereignty of the battleship, and there were those who claimed that if Sea Power was overthrown all would be chaos and anarchy. The great mass of the British people believed this to be true, and all but a few thought that Great Britain would be wise not to foster the " new-fangled flying machine." If so influential a nation as the British neglected the new instrument of war, they argued, it might never become more than a sportsman's plaything, like the balloon which for more than a century had been the amusement of the crowds and the pastime of " irresponsible aeronauts."

11

The enthusiasm of the few who did not share these views helped to save England from a sorry fate. With the barest of resources and on the most modest of incomes, small groups of officers of the Army and the Navy learned to fly—often at their own expense and without Government backing. They had realized the necessity for an air arm to support the Army and another to co-operate with the Navy. These men, not all of them young, were the founders of England's military air strength.

Unconvinced, but moved to action by the great strides made in military and naval aviation on the Continent, the British Government passed legislation creating first an Air Battalion of the Royal Engineers in 1911 and a year later the Royal Flying Corps, with a military and a naval wing.

A few far-sighted statesmen and their followers lost no opportunity for stressing the need for swift and drastic action, but their pleas had little effect.

Neither the indifference of the people, nor the meagre grants of the Government, could injure or diminish the enthusiasm and loyalty of the men who were building up the new flying Service, and to the surprise of the authorities the Army and the Navy found a ready flow of volunteers for both air and ground duties. Within a few months it had become obvious that Great Britain had an ample supply of first-class airmen and mechanics, and that if aeroplanes of good performance were made available, any smallness in numbers might be offset by the superior qualities of the machines and men should war come before the Service had reached its full peace-time stature.

But the Government tried to monopolize the business of designing and making military aeroplanes, and this limited the scope of the more enterprising private aircraft companies. The Navy, fortunately, turned to the private companies when, belatedly, it decided to make use of aeroplanes. This move put new life into the firms and broadened the country's production capacity. The Navy never fell in with the official plan to have a " unified " Air Service, and in 1914 it sought and received formal permission to call its air branch the Royal Naval Air Service.

Aeroplanes of those early days had tricks—often dangerous tricks—which were not properly understood. Some might fly for days, weeks, months and never cause their crews a moment's anxiety.

SOME EARLY TYPES

AN F.E. 2ʙ TWO-SEATER PUSHER-ENGINED BIPLANE (1914–18).

A VICKERS F.B.12 (1914–18). 100 H.P. ROTARY ENGINE.

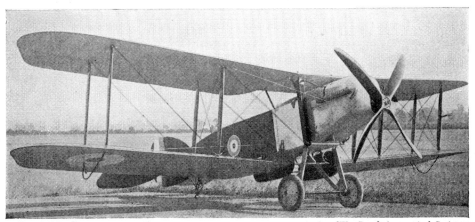

By courtesy of]   [*The Royal Aeronautical Society.*
AN EARLY TYPE OF BRISTOL FIGHTER, 1916.

SOME EARLY TYPES

BLACKBURN KANGAROO.
A large twin-engined bomber of World War I.

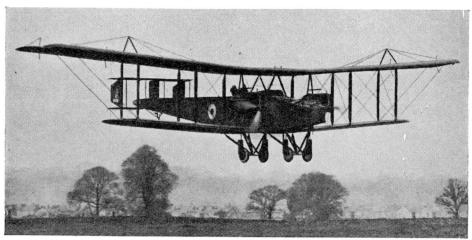

THE HANDLEY PAGE 0/400.
Built in 1916. The big British bomber of World War I.

By courtesy of]   *[The Royal Aeronautical Society.*
D.H.9A (1914–18). LIGHT BOMBER.

Others might fly well for a short time, then turn vicious ; still others might be vicious from the start and take a lot of understanding before they could be safely flown.

It soon became a " tradition " that the everyday hazards which were inseparable from the flying of such aeroplanes should be accepted by one and all. This was followed, perhaps inevitably, by the tradition that flying must continue after an accident, whatever the cause.

THE CREW OF A LINCOLN WATCH THE ARMOURER FUSING THEIR LOAD OF PRACTICE BOMBS.

In July, 1912, the Royal Flying Corps had its first fatal accident. Prudence might have required the suspension of flying until the cause was found. Instead, the order went forth that flying was to go on as though nothing had happened. Courage of a high order must have been required from the man who had to make the decision, but he insisted that, by continuing to fly, their colleagues would be honouring the dead men in the most fitting way. That " unwritten law " has been observed throughout the British military and naval air services ever since.

THE GLORIOUS TRADITION OF THE R.A.F.

Mr. Winston Churchill, then First Lord of the Admiralty, often used to fly in those early and uncertain aeroplanes, and knew from experience the risks run by " aviators "—as the flying men of those early times were called. This is what he wrote many years later :

" As I began to know more about flying I began to understand the enormous number of hazards which beset every moment of the airman's flight—(I suppose it is all different now)—and I noticed on several occasions defects in the machine which we had been flying—a broken wire, a singed wing, a cracked strut—which were the subjects of mutual congratulation between my pilot and myself once we had returned safely to terra firma. However, having been thoroughly bitten, I continued to fly on every possible occasion when my other duties permitted."

In that statement may perhaps be found the secret of that intense love of flying which made those early airmen face the unknown perils of the air as part of their normal duties. It is the admission of his " having been thoroughly bitten." Mr. Churchill was then well into the thirties, and his imagination, as he confesses, supplied him " with the most realistic anticipations of a crash."

He became interested in flying from a sense of duty and grew to love it with a passion that was later to cause others more anxiety than it gave him.

Most flyers of those times must have loved flying before they could have tasted its delights. The " bug " bit them hard and early —as it has bitten thousands since—and there came upon them a passionate yearning to venture into the air and experience the thrills and run the risks that those who stay upon the ground never know.

What type of man is it that hears and answers the call of the air ? Is he marked out and made conspicuous by some particular characteristic or personal quality. No ! The longing to fly comes to all kinds of men : the active, the quiet, the aggressive, the passive, the tall, the short, the studious and the man of action. All that is required of them is that they shall be blessed with a reasonably good physique, have their faculties in a fair state of fitness, and possess a passably good education. The good education is necessary to the military pilot—and always has been—because he must learn more than the simple movements of hand and feet needed for the controlled flight of an aeroplane.

By courtesy of]   [Messrs. Rolls-Royce Ltd.

THE HAWKER P.1052 EXPERIMENTAL JET-PLANE, A PREDECESSOR OF THE
HAWKER "HUNTER."

[*Central Press.*

FOUR-CANNON HURRICANES ON PATROL.

The leader is " peeling off " into a dive and, one by one the others will follow him.

THE GLORIOUS TRADITION OF THE R.A.F.

He is a good team man, yet can act upon his own initiative. He accepts responsibilities and takes decisions; puts a polish on his flying but never tempts providence unnecessarily. He is never too old to learn, but is a good judge of his abilities and knows when his cockpit days are over.

Military and naval flying has not yet been robbed of all its risks. It is still " spiced with danger and flavoured with peril." The timid look at the warplane with an awe tinged with fear; the adventurous with admiration tinged with longing to be master of the complex assembly of parts that give it its shape and power.

It was the adventurous men of the early twentieth century who laid the foundations of the R.A.F.'s glorious tradition; it was the adventurous men of two later generations who added new lustre to that tradition; and it is the adventurous youth of this generation who will uphold and enrich it in the coming years.

By courtesy of]   *[The Society of British Aircraft Constructors.*
A FAIREY SWORDFISH TAKING OFF FROM THE DECK OF AN AIRCRAFT CARRIER.

VICKERS SUPERMARINE SWIFT MK. IV, SWEPT-WING JET FIGHTER.
The machine in which Lt.-Commander Mike Lithgow established a new world speed record of 737·3 m.p.h. over
the Libyan desert, Tripoli, in September 1953, beating Neville Duke's record by 10·3 m.p.h.

OUR FIRST LINE OF DEFENCE

FOR centuries the Royal Navy was the bulwark upon which the people of these islands relied for their protection. The Navy is still vital to us and we should do away with it only at our peril. But it is no longer our first line of defence. That is the Royal Air Force, and if the R.A.F. is inefficient, undermanned or badly equipped when called into action, the nation would face almost certain defeat.

There are weapons of war against which none of the Services has yet found an effective defence, but history shows that sooner or later counter-measures are devised against every new weapon. Prophets foretold the end of the battleship when the submarine was invented; others foretold the end of civilization because man had learned to fly. The submarine has been, and still is, a powerful weapon but battleships still plough the seas. Aeroplanes have taken

19

heavy toll of life and property but, again, civilization continues its ceaseless processes of invention and advance.

So we may assume that means will be found for averting the worst horrors and disasters predicted for the world should war break out again and the chief weapons of attack prove to be rockets and guided missiles and not the aeroplane. If history is not misleading, we shall probably find that the aeroplane still has a big part to play in war and that, as in World War I and World War II, it will have a powerful influence on the progress of the fighting on land and sea. We shall therefore be wise, so long as the threat of war remains, to keep our Royal Air Force strong and efficient. Only when war and the threat of war have been banished will it be prudent to do away with our first line of defence.

The rise of the military aeroplane from the humble role of " scout " to its present position as the dominant arm of the Services was both spectacular and sudden. The first aeroplane flew in 1903. In 1908 the number of aeroplanes in the world began to increase rapidly. In 1909, Bleriot, a Frenchman, flying his own machine,

By courtesy of]   *[" The Aeroplane."*
A HAWKER AUDAX ARMY CO-OPERATION BIPLANE TRAILING ITS MESSAGE-PICKING-UP HOOK.

By courtesy of]   [Armstrong Whitworth Aircraft Ltd.
THE SISKIN.
An early R.A.F. post World War I fighter.

crossed the Channel and landed near Dover. That event made a far deeper impression upon the people of this country than did the historic flight of 1903. " Great Britain is no longer an island," everyone cried, and that discovery seemed to bode nothing but evil for Great Britain. The power of the Royal Navy to keep the invader out was questioned, and the possibility of finding a defence against the new weapon was doubted.

But the aeroplanes of those days were queer-looking things, made of wood, linen and wires. They were reputed to be dangerous to fly, were always going wrong, and hardly capable of carrying more than a pilot and one passenger. No wonder they were not taken seriously by the masses. As entertainment, they were good fun ; thousands of spectators used to flock to flying meetings, and the more successful " aviators " often made a good income from fees and prize money, and amassed, in addition, cartloads of trophies.

As a weapon of war the aeroplane was regarded as far too unreliable and inefficient to be of much use to the Army or to the Navy—except by a few far-sighted men and women, in and out of uniform. Yet, by 1918, the aeroplane was able to intervene

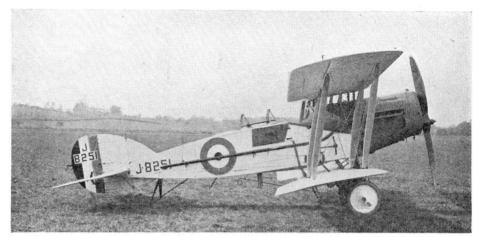

BRISTOL " FIGHTER," 1917.
Falcon-engined version, 122 m.p.h.

THE SOPWITH CAMEL.
One of the most famous warplanes of its time.

By courtesy of]   *[The Royal Aeronautical Society.*

THE SOPWITH SNIPE OF 1918.
A distant kinsman of the P1052 and P1081 jet planes of to-day.

effectively in land battles and to give valuable help in naval engagements. Whichever side had command of the air held the key to victory.

Four years earlier, military aeroplanes had been nothing more than the eyes of the Army—the aerial spy which noted the enemy's movements and brought back vital information, or directed the fire of the artillery, and in other ways aided the Army. In the first few months of World War I few were armed ; the need to fight in order to gather the information which was wanted had not arisen. Nor did they carry bombs to drop on the enemy ; hand grenades were their deadliest weapons. They were as " warlike " as a modern elementary trainer, and not nearly so fast.

That state of affairs did not last long. At first, shots were exchanged between adversaries with rifles, carbines, revolvers, automatics and even sporting guns ! Then came the machine-gun. Mounting this weapon in those slight and unsure aeroplanes was not the simple matter it is now. If the engine was in the nose, the bullets were liable to shoot off the propeller blades. If the engine was at the rear (a common place for it in those days) the machine-gun could be in the nose, but the aeroplane suffered in performance although it gave a better field of fire.

A Dutchman working for the Germans was the first to find the right answer to the machine-gun problem as it existed in those days. He invented a device which interrupted the firing of the machine-gun (which, unless deliberately checked, is automatic and continuous) so that the bullets missed the revolving blades. This allowed the Germans to have the engine in the nose and thus reap the benefit of its greater efficiency in that position.

For a time, Allied airmen suffered heavy losses because the German pilots had only to aim their aeroplanes and press the gun button. Our pilots had to try to manœuvre into positions from which they could bring their guns to bear and then to show superb judgment in their aiming. They were thus doubly handicapped.

Ultimately, the Allies adopted similar devices, and the duel between the fighters of both sides became a battle of courage and skill and a struggle for technical and operational supremacy—a struggle that produced a new type of aeroplane almost every day by both sides and a speed of development that would have seemed fantastic had it been planned, say, in the summer of 1914.

23

Back and forth went the advantage, neither side being able to hold it for long. At last, with increasing numbers of superior fighters of both private and Government manufacture, the Allied air forces gained and held the mastery until the Germans were defeated and granted an Armistice in November, 1918.

The striving for air supremacy was largely a contest between fighters—mostly single-seater fighters. Allied victory was the result of greater genius in airframe design, of bigger progress in aero-engines, of a more thorough system of training and, finally, greater skill and initiative in combat. But the margins were narrow, and a diminution of any one quality might have had the gravest consequences.

In August, 1914, when the war broke out, the bomber had not been born. By November, 1918, the Royal Air Force was using a whole range of bombers from little single-seater fighter-bombers to large four-engined aeroplanes with a range of more than a thousand miles—and had created an Independent Air Force whose duties were confined solely to bombing. Mostly, the targets were troop concentrations, railways, roads, bridges, stores and ammunition dumps behind the lines, and war factories in the industrial areas of the Saar.

Damage to targets like these helped the Allied cause. It delayed enemy troops on their way to the front, and repairs diverted men and materials from other work ; it destroyed precious resources ; the destruction of an ammunition dump might cause the postponement of a planned offensive against a weak spot in the Allied lines. Bombs on a war factory might deprive the enemy of weapons or equipment he might be urgently in need of. In this manner, as well as in direct attacks on the enemy in the sky and in and around the fighting fronts, the aeroplane became a most potent instrument of warfare.

In its conviction that Air Power, whether it be military or naval, was a single power, the British Government took the momentous step of amalgamating the Royal Flying Corps and the Royal Naval Air Service while the war still raged, and at a time when Allied fortunes were none too bright. The date of amalgamation was 1st April, 1918. The single Service was known as the Royal Air Force, the name it keeps to-day. In 1924, a Fleet Air Arm branch of the R.A.F. was formed but in 1937 it was transferred to the Admiralty and given a new name. To-day, however, the old name of Fleet Air Arm is in use again.

BRISTOL BEAUFORTS.
These were used for various duties—bombing and torpedo attack.

Although the Government reduced the R.A.F. to but one-tenth of its war-time strength at the end of the war, they placed upon it many responsibilities, some of a kind never before entrusted to an air force. One of the more onerous lay in keeping order in mandated territories where banditry and lawlessness had been rife for centuries, and where peace was always precarious and dependent upon local expeditionary forces and garrisons.

The Royal Air Force brought to bear a new kind of pressure and, with experience, was able to maintain law and order without

A WESTLAND LYSANDER ARMY CO-OPERATION PLANE.
As used by the R.A.F. in 1939.

inflicting heavy casualties on the troublesome tribesmen or suffering losses themselves. Often, the mere threat of air action was sufficient to check an uprising, and regions long accustomed to the periodical raids of hillmen and warlike tribes of the desert lived in peace and prosperity under the watchful guardianship of the Royal Air Force.

If the trouble was of a kind not suitable for air action, the Royal Air Force would fly armed soldiers to the scene in its big troop transports. In 1929, it rescued scores of civilians from Kabul, capital of Afghanistan, whose lives had been imperilled by an uprising. Earlier, it had hunted down the Mad Mullah, a powerful chieftain who had terrorized the industrious and peace-loving people of Somaliland, and driven him out of the country.

It gave much help, too, in the surveying and opening of air communications between England and South Africa and between England and Australia. For many months it ran a regular air mail service across the desert between Cairo (Egypt) and Basra (Iraq), and undertook many a survey flight and many a " proving " flight over routes to be flown later by commercial airliners. Its contributions to the development of our Commonwealth system of air communications, indeed, are larger than is generally known.

The squadrons overseas had, of course, to be constantly changing their officers and men, and every year troopships would leave England for Egypt, Iraq (once known as Mesopotamia—or " Mespot " for short), India and Singapore. Some of the luckier aircrews were able to fly out to their new stations—as, for instance, when a squadron of flying-boats took-off from the R.A.F. marine base near Plymouth and flew to Australia before returning to Singapore, where it was to be stationed.

At home, in England, the smallness of the Royal Air Force was, to some extent, offset by the high standards set and the terms of service offered. Only the best of the candidates who offered their services could be taken. The tests which were set varied according to the branch or trade in which the candidate wished to serve, and were strictly enforced.

The peace-time efficiency of the Royal Air Force was no myth, no legendary tale, but something very real and substantial. From 1920 to 1937, the Royal Air Force staged a public parade every year, and showed its skill in all branches of military flying. This " pageant " was held at Hendon Airfield, one of the oldest flying

By courtesy of]   [" Flight."
BRISTOL BLENHEIM BOMBER.
The first type of bomber to fly an operational sortie in World War II.

BRISTOL BEAUFIGHTER.
" Whispering Death " was the name the Japanese gave to the Bristol Beaufighter when it went into service in the
Far East.

centres in this country. The programme differed every year, but the thousands of spectators who thronged to see it used to watch a flying spectacle which no other air force in the world could have equalled. Its superb flying won the R.A.F. so much admiration that people betrayed no alarm at its diminished squadrons. " An air force that can fly like that," they argued, " can lick all-comers."

Thousands who would like to have seen the Royal Air Force on parade could not afford the time and money to travel all the way to Hendon. Then, in 1934, came the first of six Empire Air Days, which were celebrated on or around 24th May—Empire Day. On these days, scores of R.A.F. stations were thrown open, and the public were given the opportunity of making a closer and more intimate acquaintance not only with the officers and airman on the station but with all the innumerable technicalities of life in the R.A.F. The aeroplanes were put on show for people to inspect with great thoroughness. Visitors were allowed to sit in cockpits, to move controls, and everything was explained in great detail. In the hangars and workshops, displays of aircraft instruments and equipment were arranged. Only the very secret things were kept under lock and key.

There were flying displays, too. If the nature of one station's work did not allow it to put on a very spectacular flying programme, another station would send over a flight of fighters or light bombers and make the day more exciting for the guests. In this way, people could be assured of getting both entertainment and instruction wherever they went.

It fell to the lot of the peace-time R.A.F. to score a great international triumph—that of winning outright for Great Britain the coveted Jacques Schneider Seaplane Trophy, which had been put up for competition in 1913. Great Britain had won the Trophy in 1914 (at a speed of 86·8 miles an hour) and again in 1922 (at a speed of 145·7 miles an hour). By then the cost of competing was going up by leaps and bounds (the aeroplanes were getting faster and were growing increasingly expensive to build and fly), and the outlay was more than private individuals and firms could afford. But such was the prestige to be derived from winning the prize that governments began to take a hand and enter teams. In 1927, the British Government sent an R.A.F. team to Italy (the winner of the previous contest) and the Trophy came back to England, having been won at an average speed of 281·68 miles an hour.

By courtesy of]   [*Boulton Paul Aircraft Ltd.*

DEFIANT.

Although the Defiant had a short operational life, it won undying fame over Dunkirk in 1940 by shooting down a flight of Nazi fighters in a single engagement.

There was no race in 1928. In 1929, the contest was held in British waters. Again an R.A.F. team represented Great Britain, and again Great Britain won the Trophy, this time at an average of 328·63 miles an hour. The next, and what proved to be the last, contest for the Trophy took place in British waters in 1931, and for the third time Great Britain was represented by the R.A.F. On this occasion, the cost was borne by a wealthy patriot, Lady Houston, after the Government had declined, on the score of expense, to foot the bill. Lady Houston's generous act was well rewarded. The British team won for the third successive time and, under the regulations of the contest, the Trophy became Great Britain's property. It is a finely executed work of art depicting a winged figure kissing the waves, and now has an honoured place in the Royal Aero Club.

The Royal Air Force also set up a number of international air records between 1919 and 1939, including two long-distance records, three absolute height records for aeroplanes, and two absolute speed records. Although giving public displays, taking part in international air races and making new records are not, strictly speaking, military duties, the R.A.F. Display, Empire Air Day, the Schneider Trophy contests and the international records all go to prove that the peace-time R.A.F. of 1919–39, although small, was of the highest quality in men and machines.

By courtesy of]   [*A. V. Roe & Co., Ltd.*

THE AVRO 707, which because its wings form an equilateral triangle is known as the " Delta," in flight.

[*By courtesy of Vickers-Armstrongs, Ltd.*

THE VICKERS VALIANT, BRITAIN'S FIRST FOUR-JET BOMBER.
Powered by four Rolls-Royce Avons.

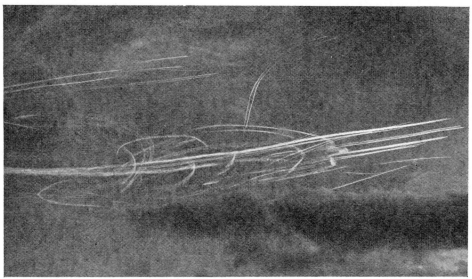

VAPOUR TRAILS IN THE SKY.
Fighters intercepting a formation of bombers.

THE BATTLE THAT CHANGED THE COURSE OF HISTORY

WHEN the R.A.F. celebrated its last Empire Air Day it was being expanded rapidly, and the war clouds over Europe were growing darker. The Government were trying to make good in the shortest time possible the shortages resulting from their example in disarmament. Germany, forbidden to possess an air force by the peace treaties of 1919, had for years resorted to every trick and stratagem to re-build her aircraft industry and her air force, and when the Nazis came to power in 1933 they had a big, thriving aircraft industry and an organization that needed only uniform and symbols to turn it into an air force. Within a few years, Germany had the Luftwaffe—the new name for her air force—" in being," and

By courtesy of] [*The Society of British Aircraft Constructors.*
SPITFIRES OFF TO INTERCEPT THE ENEMY.

was planning to give it duties and responsibilities beyond any that fell to air forces in the 1914–18 War.

World War II started on 1st September, 1939. Germany attacked Poland, and Great Britain, France and the Commonwealth countries declared war on Germany. The race between the R.A.F. and the Luftwaffe had been won by the Luftwaffe, and the output of German warplane factories, arsenals and training schools at that time was greater than that from those of Great Britain. It was perhaps fortunate that Germany was not ready to fight the nations which had declared war on her. The declarations had taken her by surprise—in spite of the repeated warnings that Great Britain and her allies would fight if Germany attacked Poland—and Germany had to re-make her war plans.

The test did not come until 1940. Early in the spring of that year Germany invaded and occupied Norway, then swept upon Holland and Belgium, and drove westward into France. Her successes had a text-book precision about them, and by the end of June all the invaded countries had been knocked out of the fight. Only Great Britain remained. We stood alone with the enemy facing us

VICKERS "VALIANT" LONG-RANGE FOUR-JET MEDIUM BOMBER.

along a coastline that stretched from the northern tip of Norway to the most westerly point of France, with a strip of water only 21 miles wide at its narrowest separating us from the victorious German armies.

We had, too, a new enemy, Italy, who, seeing the prospect of rich spoils for little effort, had thrown her lot in with Germany.

To the rest of the world Great Britain's plight must have seemed forlorn. But under the inspiring leadership of their new Prime Minister, Mr. Winston Churchill—who perhaps more than any other statesman of that time understood the role that the R.A.F. was to play—the people of Great Britain prepared to meet the impact of German military might.

There was an ominous pause as the Germans made ready for their biggest adventure. Never before had the Luftwaffe acted independently. Now, it had to win and hold command of the air over a corner of England so firmly that German legions might cross the Channel in boats or by air and set foot securely upon the land they had to conquer or leave as a constant threat to their earlier conquests.

By courtesy of]   [*The Society of British Aircraft Constructors.*

MOSQUITOS BOMBING AN IMPORTANT TARGET IN A DARING DAYLIGHT RAID.

THE BATTLE THAT CHANGED THE COURSE OF HISTORY

Its opening tactics suggested that the Luftwaffe was none too sure of itself. Instead of launching a tremendous offensive with the object of paralysing the south-east corner where the invasion was to start, it began attacking convoys in the Channel. No doubt to its surprise, every attack was challenged by the R.A.F., and the Luftwaffe had to fight its way through to its targets. Moreover, it had to pay far more dearly for its successes than its leaders had expected.

[*Central Press.*

FIGHTER PILOTS RUNNING TO THEIR MACHINES ON RECEIPT OF RAIDERS WARNING.

The Germans could not withdraw from their set purpose. They were committed to the invasion of the British Isles and invade it they must. So the Luftwaffe, mounting increasingly heavy sorties, began its methodically planned assault by hitting at coastal towns, then gradually bringing the fighter stations within their forays, with the object of driving the Royal Air Force out of the invasion area, and setting up that mastery of the air which was vital to the success of the German scheme.

[*War Artists & Illustrators*.

SPITFIRES DESTROYING ENEMY PLANES IN AN ATTACK ON A NAZI
FORMATION.

One goes crashing down, while another has had its flap controls shot away.

Deeper and deeper they struck inland. Fighter airfields north as well as south of the Thames were bombed. Buildings were blown sky-high, the landing areas pocketed with bomb craters, operations rooms wrecked, communication lines severed, fuel stores fired, but still Fighter Command fought back ; still the raiders were intercepted and fiercely punished.

Every trick the Luftwaffe's commanders could practise was tried. Decoy raids were staged, sometimes two or three simultaneously, in the hope that the defenders would be lured away from the main target of the day and the way to it opened. Fighter protection for the raiding bombers was increased. It seemed that if Fighter Command could not be blasted out of existence it must be overwhelmed by sheer weight of numbers.

Systematically, every raid, feint or purposeful, was met. Often the odds were ten to one against the defenders, but their interceptions were so precise and pressed home with such vigour and valour that the Luftwaffe would often break formation in confusion, scatter their bombs at random and make for home. The encounters were usually brief and perilous, though many a fleeing enemy was chased and shot down far from the point of interception. Often the progress of the battle was inscribed on the sky in long, intertwining vapour trails, like those in the photograph on page 31.

Fearful of failure, the Germans clung to their planned offensive, and at the scheduled time, with Fighter Command still robust and resolute and showing little outward evidence of its grim ordeal, the Luftwaffe turned upon London. Day and night they came, starting great fires, wiping out factories, offices and homes in a bid to paralyse the city. But London " took it " and carried on.

As that memorable summer of 1940, with its long warm days and clear skies, gave way to autumn the Germans realized that their invasion plans were wrecked. The defenders could neither be defeated in combat nor overwhelmed by numbers. Nor could the Luftwaffe parry the harassing and disrupting counter-thrusts by aeroplanes of Bomber and Coastal Commands and of the Fleet Air Arm, whose frequent visits to the Channel ports of Belgium and France played havoc with the orderly rows of invasion barges and impeded the careful rehearsals which were so necessary to the success of an adventure of such magnitude and moment.

Their realization of failure was the signal for the start of a new

THE BATTLE OF BRITAIN MEMORIAL WINDOW, WESTMINSTER ABBEY.

offensive—the Battle of the Night Skies. Its objective was to dislocate the life of every large town in the British Isles, to destroy war factories and to break the resistance of the people. The story of that testing period, too, is woven large and bright into the fabric of the R.A.F.'s history. It was, in a way, an epilogue to the Battle of Britain.

But historians of all future time will say that the Battle of Britain was the R.A.F.'s most glorious achievement. They will be careful to record the parts played by thousands who neither flew nor serviced a fighter in that momentous struggle, nor plotted a raider's course, nor scanned a radar screen, loaded, aimed or fired an anti-aircraft gun, nor manned a barrage balloon site, yet whose share in the victory cannot be denied. They may marvel, as we still marvel, that so few squadrons could have inflicted so resounding a defeat upon an air force superior in numbers, fortified by recent successes, and animated by a fanatical belief in the cause it was serving. But it was defeated in an encounter that will always be classed as one of the battles that changed the course of history.

[*Fox Photos.*

FIGHTER PILOTS RESTING BETWEEN COMBATS.
A scene at a fighter station during the Battle of Britain.

A LINCOLN BOMBER OF THE EMPIRE TEST PILOTS SCHOOL SILHOUETTED AGAINST
THE SETTING SUN.

WINGS OF VICTORY

HOW dramatically the Battle of Britain had changed the course of history soon became clear. Almost nightly, raiders were over England but the daytime skies were quiet. The squadrons of Fighter Command which for three months had known little rest now found time hanging heavily. The enemy would risk no second daylight encounter with them for fear of a second defeat. To make them fight they would need to be challenged in their own air across the Channel.

Thus began a series of " sweeps " which, as the months rolled by and the Royal Air Force grew in stature, involved aerial fleets matching in size the enemy armadas which had tried to pave the way for a German invasion of Great Britain. With heavier armament than the eight ·303-in. machine-guns with which they had broken and scattered the Luftwaffe's hordes, they swooped upon the enemy in those areas of the Continent which were within their range. Soon, to give greater weight and significance to their offensive, the fighters had turned themselves into fighter-bombers, and their pilots became expert marksmen, picking off small but important targets with remarkable precision. Later, to bring more distant targets within their range, extra fuel tanks were fitted to the wings—tanks which could be thrown away if a fight broke out and full fighter manœuvrability was needed.

At first, no fights broke out. The Luftwaffe allowed the R.A.F. to make their sweeps without let or hindrance. To have accepted the challenge would have been too costly in men and material. But when, finding no one to dispute their way through the skies, the R.A.F. taunted the Luftwaffe by shooting up its airfields, its barracks, headquarters and stores, by knocking out locomotives, and shooting up road convoys, the enemy had to fight back, if only to preserve the morale of the Luftwaffe and of the soldiers of the " occupation " forces. Usually, clashes occurred only when the Luftwaffe could muster a superior force, and the Germans began to rely more and more upon anti-aircraft guns to take toll of the invaders and to divert them from their purpose.

Light twin-engined bombers were added to the fighter sweeps, and the R.A.F.'s daylight offensive against the enemy in the occupied countries gradually assumed the proportions of a major operation, and grew until the enemy was being harassed somewhere day and night every day on which the weather was " flyable." Was it any wonder that the Germans had made so desperate and costly a bid to add Great Britain to the list of occupied countries ?

As the Allied air offensive against the enemy in the occupied countries grew in weight and intensity so, too, did the onslaught against his war production centres—the great industrial areas of the Ruhr, the big railway marshalling yards, the armament factories in Berlin and elsewhere, the great synthetic oil plants, engineering works making diesel engines for submarines, the shipyards where submarines were made, the research centres, the fugitive cruisers and battleships seeking means of escape into the open seas to join in the war against Allied ships. The bombers used against these more distant targets grew not only in numbers ; they grew, too, in size, range and lifting capacity, until at the close of the war, bombs each weighing more than ten tons were causing destruction unimaginable in 1939.

A HUDSON OF COASTAL COMMAND. [*Crown Copyright Reserved.*]

One of several types of American warplanes which were flown by R.A.F. crews.

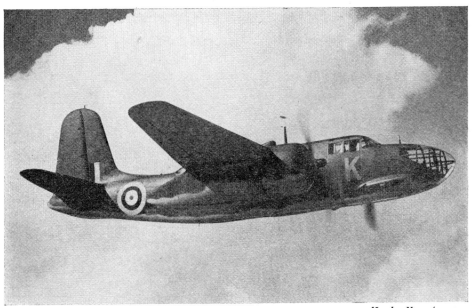

BOSTON TWIN-ENGINED LIGHT BOMBER. [*London News Agency.*]

Another American type flown by the R.A.F. A night-fighter version of this was known as the Havoc.

This mighty growth of air power and its use against the enemy would perhaps have been slower, and would certainly have taken a different course if R.A.F. Fighter Command had not followed up its brilliant victory in the Battle of Britain with another triumph. When the Luftwaffe was driven from the daylight skies of England and turned to night bombing, the R.A.F. had few properly equipped night-fighter squadrons, and those available used methods of interception no different, basically, from those in use in World War I. The aeroplanes could be directed by radio to the vicinity of a raider, but the crews had to rely upon searchlights to pick up targets for them. Their chances of making contact in the wide dark sky were small.

But when the Luftwaffe turned to night raiding, the R.A.F. was receiving the first of a new type of fighter equipped with a special device which enabled crews to pick up the enemy without the aid of searchlights. More will be said about this device in a later chapter. It is only necessary here to record that week by week the enemy's losses grew and grew until night raids on England became as unprofitable as the raids made by daylight had been. Within eight months the enemy's casualties had reached a figure that might have brought the Luftwaffe's night offensive to a halt even if Germany had not, at that moment, decided to transfer many squadrons to the East to take part in the opening attack on Russia. From time to time during the next four years the enemy resumed its night raids against the British Isles, but never with the ferocity or on the scale of the night raids of 1940/41.

Nearly every raid was a costly business, and the interceptors' success made it obvious that darkness was no longer the protective cloak for the night bomber which it had been in the 1914–18 War and the early months of the Second World War.

Japan Comes In

In December, 1941, the Japanese struck the treacherous blow that brought the United States into the war on the side of Great Britain and her Allies. Without warning, she bombed the great U.S. naval base at Pearl Harbour in the Hawaiian Islands, at the same time opening land and sea campaigns that carried her conquests deep into the Pacific and the greater part of the Far East, and even into India itself, before they were halted.

[*Central Press.*

A TWIN-ENGINED AVRO MANCHESTER.

This type in 1942 was the R.A.F.'s newest and most efficient bomber. It was replaced by the famous four-engined Lancaster.

Japan's action opened a vast new theatre of war and added to Great Britain's burdens. Nevertheless, it brought the full weight of the United States into the war, and before many months had passed

AN AVRO LINCOLN BOMBER IN WAR-TIME CAMOUFLAGE.

43

the British Isles became an "unsinkable aircraft carrier," dotted with hundreds of air bases from which, in ever-increasing strength, went great swarms of bombers, American and British, to wage a continuous day-and-night offensive and to give the enemy no respite or chance to repair the devastation done by the constant deluge of bombs.

Meanwhile, both the Royal Air Force and the United States Army Air Forces steadily increased the scale of the support they gave to the armies fighting the Germans and Italians, and those

By courtesy of]   [The Consolidated Aircraft Corporation.
CATALINA LONG-RANGE FLYING-BOAT OF COASTAL COMMAND.

opposing the Japanese. The navies of both countries, too, likewise struck at the enemy with blows from the air that increased in effect every day.

The squadrons assigned to the armies had work to do of a kind quite different from that done by the squadrons which worked independently. They had to follow methods and adopt tactics similar to those brought to such a high state of effectiveness by the Luftwaffe in its early campaigns, and they soon proved that they were as efficient in co-operating with land forces as they were when playing the role of an independent Service and hitting the enemy hard and telling blows without direct help from either army or navy.

Historians are satisfied that the destruction by bombing of

Photos by courtesy of]   [*Boeing Aircraft Company.*

FOUR-ENGINE FLYING FORTRESS B-17C.

Two pictures, showing overhead and underneath views. These machines had a top speed well in excess of 300 m.p.h.
and were specially equipped for high-altitude operation.

BEAUFIGHTER.

A radar-equipped night fighter which won a splendid reputation in the Second World War.

Germany's principal armament centres was a major contribution to her downfall. She could not repair as quickly as the Allies destroyed, and slowly output fell below need, with the inevitable consequence that her air force, her army and her navy all suffered shortages which impaired their efficiency and striking power.

The Air War at Sea

The longest and bitterest battle of the war was fought on and above the ten million square miles of the Atlantic Ocean, that vast arena where the Germans made their desperate bid to stop the movement of vital supplies over the main sea lanes of the world. The enemy had remembered his near-success in World War I with fleets of submarines and surface ships and in his second attempt he used the same methods on a larger scale with more efficient weapons.

The submarines were larger, had more range and were more numerous. The surface ships—battleships and cruisers—were faster, more heavily armed and more difficult to sink. By overwhelming France the Germans secured excellent ports from which their under-water craft had direct access to the Atlantic and were saved a hazardous journey through the English Channel or round the north of Scotland. The enemy made good use, too, of aeroplanes in his war on shipping—for direct attack, for directing submarines to convoys, and for the interception of Allied bombers on anti-submarine patrol.

WINGS OF VICTORY

Within a few hours of Great Britain's declaration of war enemy submarines and surface ships were at work. Submarines were the last of the enemy's forces to stop fighting. During the whole of the war's six years there had been no pause and neither ships nor aircraft engaged in the defence of Allied shipping enjoyed a moment's relaxation. From bases extending from Iceland to Africa the ceaseless struggle went on, with both sides steadily increasing the number and efficiency of their weapons.

Beyond the range of land-based aeroplanes, the brunt of the air side of the battle was borne by carrier aircraft of the Fleet Air Arm ; from land and marine bases it was the Coastal Command of the Royal Air Force that spread protective wings over the convoys and prevented the wholesale destruction which surface ships and shipborne aircraft, unaided, could not have averted.

Atlantic weather is notoriously stormy, and tranquil moments are rare. The weather, indeed, was the airman's biggest enemy and aircrews of Coastal Command had to contend as a matter of routine with conditions that often stopped all other flying. German submarines and surface ships sank thousands of tons of Allied shipping, but they failed to break even one of the several " life-lines " which linked the sources of war supplies with the various theatres where war was waged. Coastal Command alone claimed the sinking of

By courtesy of]   [Handley Page Ltd.
THE HALIFAX.
A big bomber of World War II.

47

196 German submarines (22 shared with surface forces) and damaged another 293. On one occasion a Coastal Command aircrew " captured " an enemy submarine, and wrote a special little chapter all for itself in the history of warfare.

As always, the war was brought to an end by soldiers and sailors. Some historians claim that Japan was beaten by the two atomic bombs which the United States Air Forces dropped on Hiroshima and Nagasaki, but the rolling back of Japanese conquests had begun long before those fateful events, and the result of the war in the Pacific seemed to be a foregone conclusion. The only uncertainty appeared to be the time that Japan could hold out against the advancing Allied Forces.

However, no one disputes the dominant part played by the aeroplane. It became the decisive weapon in every clash between the opposing forces in which aeroplanes could intervene, and almost invariably, the side which could put its bombers, its fighters, its fighter-bombers, its torpedo-aircraft, its paratroop transports and its airborne-force gliders to best use claimed the victory.

FAIREY FIREFLY NAVAL FIGHTER.

CURVES AND STRAIGHT LINES GIVE THE CANBERRA JET BOMBER A DISTINCTIVE SILHOUETTE.

SOME FAMOUS R.A.F. PLANES

THE British Government had the best of intentions when they set up a national factory to design and build aeroplanes for the Royal Flying Corps. They argued that the Army and the Navy would be able to say exactly what sort of aeroplanes they needed and the factory would be able to supply them. That was good in theory but bad in practice. The older Services stressed the qualities they deemed most desirable, and an aeroplane which gave the observer a broad view of the ground so that nothing on the surface was hidden from him, or one which was " stable " in flight and formed a better gun platform, found readier approval than one which gave the pilot a wide view of the sky, or which flew fast, or was manœuvrable.

Thus, Government-built aeroplanes suffered from a grave handicap, and when air scouting grew into air warfare, Royal Flying Corps pilots found themselves outclassed by opponents with aeroplanes of superior performance and fighting power. The insistence upon " military " qualities in the early Government-built aeroplane was, in some measure, a cause of the setback suffered by the R.F.C. when forced to fight for the privilege of watching and reporting enemy movements and dispositions.

Admiralty orders had been rather less specific in the qualities required from naval aeroplanes, and the private firms which supplied them had greater freedom to design for performance. When the 1914–18 War broke out, more than one designer had already shown evidence of the skill and genius which, in the following thirty-odd years, profoundly influenced the warplane's development.

By courtesy of]   [The Society of British Aircraft Constructors.
AN AUSTER AIR-OBSERVATION PLANE COMING IN TO LAND.

Not all the aeroplanes flown by the British Air Service squadrons and training schools have been British-designed or British-built. In World War I we had at first to rely upon the French for some of our designs and for a great many of our aero-engines. In World War II (and for a similar reason) we had to turn to the United States. Governments in both times had failed to see the nearness of war and, when it came, our own resources and manufacturing capacity were too small to satisfy our needs.

Scores of different aeroplanes were built in World War I, some in large numbers, some in twos and threes. None, perhaps, was made in such large numbers as the Avro 504. This was a pre-war design and was ordered by the Admiralty for the R.N.A.S. It had two seats, arranged tandem-wise, was a biplane and was distinguished

A FLIGHT OF BARRACUDA TORPEDO-BOMBERS DIVING TO THE ATTACK.

by an exceptionally long fuselage and small tail surfaces. The R.N.A.S. promptly used it for bombing attacks on enemy airship sheds and other important targets.

Its belligerent (or operational) life was comparatively short but its active life lasted all through the war and for ten years afterwards. Indeed, an Avro 504 was reported to be flying in Australia in 1939 —with its original rotary engine! If the report was true, this particular aeroplane must have been the longest-lived in the world —outside of a museum. Another, reconditioned for the occasion, flew at the 1950 R.A.F. Display.

The 504 survived because it proved to be the finest trainer of its time. Wood for its construction came from Canada by the shipload. Scores of factories were turned over to making 504 parts; scores more to putting them together. After the war, hundreds were disposed of as surplus and from 1919 onwards thousands of people had their first taste of flying in Avro 504s.

Every peace-time R.A.F. airfield had its quota, too, and with only a change of engine (radial for rotary) and a change of letter

BRISTOL BRIGAND.
A kinsman of the famous Beaufighter.

SOME FAMOUS R.A.F. PLANES

AN AVRO-ANSON 20 TWIN-ENGINED TRAINER.

after its number (N for K) it remained the R.A.F.'s standard elementary trainer until 1926 or 1927. Its amazing antics when flown
by a skilful " aerobatic " pilot used to amuse and thrill spectators at
the early Hendon Pageants. They called it " crazy flying," and crazy
it was.

One R.A.F. fighter to win lasting fame was the Sopwith Camel.
This lively little single-seater came to the squadrons with a reputation—a not too pleasant reputation. It was reported to spin without warning and to kill its pilots. It certainly needed understanding,
but once they learned its tricks pilots became devoted to it and
wanted to fly no other aeroplane. It was fast for those days, with
a top speed of 120 miles an hour, a good climb, and two machine-
guns synchronized to fire through the airscrew. Pilots who flew
Camels acquired a prestige which raised them above the common
level; they were regarded with a respect bordering upon hero-
worship.

Late in the war came another famous Sopwith fighter—the Snipe
—as the Camel's successor. The Snipe had a better all-round
performance, as was only natural, but it was not so lively as the
Camel and required more vigorous handling in aerobatics. It marked
the beginning of a new era in fighters because it called for more
thinking from the pilot. With earlier fighters, pilot and machine
had been one, as a good rider and his horse are one and move in

harmony. The trend started by the Snipe continues to this day: the pilot must fly his fighter, not ride it as in the early days.

Another distinguished fighter was the S.E.5, said to be the only outstanding aeroplane that was designed by the Government factory. It was widely used in action and probably did more fighting than any other type of World War I. It lacked the agility of the Camel and Snipe, but it was fast, could climb to a great height, was easy to fly, and so well made that pilots would dive it steeply without wondering if the wings would fold up when they flattened out. At one Hendon Pageant a flight of S.E.5As gave a display of aerobatics in formation that was easily the most spectacular item in the programme, and was talked about for months afterwards. Never had so daring an exhibition of flying been attempted anywhere in the world.

Yet another notable warplane that won bright and enduring fame was the Bristol Fighter. This entered the arena when the fortunes of the Allied air forces were at a low ebb. The Germans had gained the lead and the R.F.C. was fighting desperately to " keep its tail up." The Bristol Fighter changed the situation. Here was a two-seater that was fast, a good climber, compact and unencumbered by useless equipment, and—virtue above all virtues—capable of shooting at an enemy from front or rear. The pilot had a fixed gun firing forward through the airscrew disc ; the observer had a free gun which he could swing through a wide arc. This was a weapon with which to tackle any odds. It was, at that time, like two fighters in one, and it did more than any other aeroplane to wrest the command of the air from the Germans and to prevent their ever regaining it.

Squadrons first had the Bristol Fighter in the spring of 1917, and such were its merits that it remained in front-line service with the Royal Air Force for nearly ten years after the war ended. It was one of those rare creations—the right type of aeroplane at the right time. It will always hold a high place in the R.A.F.'s history.

Closely resembling the Bristol Fighter was the D.H.9A, a bomber which was derived from the D.H.9 although not much like it. The D.H.9A was largely used by the Independent Air Force for raids on German towns. It had one gun firing forward through the airscrew disc, and two free guns on a mounting which allowed them to be swung as a single unit through a wide field of fire. It was also notable in having an American engine, the Liberty, the first and only

SOME FAMOUS R.A.F. PLANES

A FAIREY BARRACUDA SHIP-BORNE PLANE.

British aeroplane of World War I so equipped. The D.H.9A, like the Bristol Fighter, remained in service with the Royal Air Force for some ten years after the war ended.

The R.A.F.'s first specially designed night bomber was the twin-engined Handley Page O/100. The plans for this " outsize aeroplane " were submitted to the Admiralty. By a stroke of good fortune the project came before a naval officer who, like Mr. Churchill, his chief, had been bitten by the aviation bug, and he, seeing the advantages to be derived from an aeroplane which could carry a heavy load of bombs and drop them on the factories which fed the German Army, Navy and Air Force, at once urged the production of the O/100 for the Royal Naval Air Service.

In the utmost secrecy the new bomber took shape, and when tested was found to be " up to specification." It was unfortunate that on a delivery flight to France one of the first to be built was landed on the wrong side of the lines and fell, undamaged, into the hands of the enemy. After forty O/100s had been delivered an improved version, the O/400, went into production, and it was this version that became the standard " heavy bomber " of the British Air Services. The O/400 was a " slow, stately ship," and in its drab olive camouflage it looked a veritable giant to eyes not accustomed to the sight of aeroplanes of such massive proportions. Size was

SOME FAMOUS R.A.F. PLANES

A TYPHOON FIGHTER.
A fast and ferocious interceptor.

[Associated Press.

not its only distinguishing feature ; it had an engine note character-istically its own : a deep uneven throbbing as the engines fell into and out of phase through lack of synchronization.

While the Handley Page factories were busy making O/400s the drawing office was designing a still larger bomber. This had four engines and a range of more than a thousand miles. It was the most ambitious landplane project ever attempted in Great Britain at that time. It was called the Handley Page V/1500, and four were being made ready to bomb Berlin when the Armistice was signed. London was within easy striking distance of German continental air bases, but Berlin was some 600 miles from the nearest Royal Air Force base. Therefore the V/1500s would have needed the protection of the long, dark nights that come only in the middle of December if they were to avoid the risk of daylight interception. The war ended in November. No doubt the operation would have been carefully rehearsed before it was embarked upon, but everyone knew that the chances of survival were small. Yet there was no lack of volunteers. Every V/1500 could have been manned a dozen times over !

We have found room to mention briefly only eight of the scores of aeroplanes which saw active service with the Royal Flying Corps, the Royal Naval Air Service and the Royal Air Force in World War I. So many more deserve comment : the Bleriot monoplane,

SOME FAMOUS R.A.F. PLANES

Maurice Farman Longhorn, the Henri Farman, the line of B.E.s, R.E.s, S.E.s F.E.s (from the National factory), the Morane Parasol, Morane Biplane, Sopwith Tabloid, Pup, Triplane, Baby, Dolphin, Nieuport Scout, Martinsyde Elephant, Bristol D Scout, the Bristol Monoplane, the Spad, at least half a dozen D.H. types—the list is almost endless. Luckily, others have written about these World War I aeroplanes, and you can still find books that describe them, as well as the eight we have described, in more detail than is possible here.

PEACE-TIME WARPLANES

For the first five years of peace, the Royal Air Force was using up its huge war-time stock of aeroplanes and few new types were built. From 1924 onwards, two or three—sometimes half a dozen —new types appeared every year, but few of them saw squadron service. The Royal Air Force was small and its needs were meagre. The system under which six, eight or even ten different types were built every year had the advantage of keeping all the aircraft firms " on their toes " and their design staffs alert. Business in the aircraft industry at that time was none too brisk, and a contract from the

By courtesy of]   [" Flight."

HANDLEY PAGE HASTINGS.
Largely used by Transport Command.

Air Ministry was a prize worth striving for. The competition thus fostered kept British warplanes ahead of all others.

That explains, in part, why those types accepted by the Royal Air Force were so often accepted also by other air forces. The competition was so fierce that the Air Ministry was able to set almost " impossible " specifications—that is, call for a performance which, on paper, seemed unattainable. Yet, how often the aircraft firm beat the specification ! Often, too, the manufacturer produced an aeroplane of his own design and to his own specification which was better than that specified by the Air Ministry. These aeroplanes were known as " private ventures " because the companies which made them acted on their own initiative and took all the risks of failure. But success, not failure, was their usual reward.

By 1918 the biplane had gained a firm supremacy over the monoplane and many years were to elapse before it was effectively challenged by the monoplane. Its decline began in the early 1930s but it survived in the Royal Air Force and the Royal Navy until well into 1949.

If, as some claim, the Royal Air Force was frequently in a state of active service when exercising its guardianship of turbulent regions, the types of aeroplane used by the " active service " squadrons deserve fuller recognition than is usually accorded to peace-time types. Nevertheless, the odds were so much in favour of the airmen that the principal tests of their aeroplanes revolved largely round the reliability of the engines and an ability to clear fairly high mountain ranges.

Outstanding types designed between the wars which had no " operational life " in World War II include the Siskin, Bulldog, Fury and Gauntlet fighters ; the Virginia, Sidestrand, Horsley, Fox, Hart, Heyford and Harrow bombers ; the Atlas, Wapiti, Audax, Wallace, Fawn and Hector army co-operation types ; the Scapa, Singapore, Southampton, Rangoon, London, Stranraer and Lerwick flying-boats, and the Dart, Firefly, Gordon, Shark and Flycatcher of the Fleet Air Arm. These, with trainers and troop transports, were the actors who, in their heyday, took the stage at Hendon and enthralled the crowds in the packed enclosures. But they won no medals.

Great Britain's belated rearmament began, half-heartedly, in 1935 ; a year earlier the Hawker Aircraft Company had completed

By courtesy of]   [De Havilland Aircraft Co. Ltd.

CHIPMUNK TWO-SEATER BASIC TRAINERS AS USED BY THE RESERVE SQUADRONS.

the design of an aeroplane which was to make history. This was the Hurricane, the R.A.F.'s first monoplane fighter since World War I and its first eight-gun fighter. Such were the merits of the Hurricane that no fewer than sixteen foreign countries had placed orders for it, and six of them acquired the licence to build it, before the war began !

The Hurricane was the central figure in what we might call " an industrial drama " long before it became the hero of a grim battle. Convinced that the storm gathering over Europe would break, sooner or later, Hawker's invested a vast sum of money in plant, materials and machinery in order that they could produce at least a thousand Hurricanes—a number far beyond the total ordered for the Royal Air Force. Later, the Air Ministry endorsed Hawker's action by placing a far more substantial order than the original.

While the R.A.F.'s fighter squadrons were being armed with their new eight-gun monoplane, a second eight-gun fighter was being designed at another factory—that of Vickers-Supermarine. This was to be the Hurricane's doughty partner in the Battle of Britain —the immortal Spitfire.

The Hurricane looked, and was, rugged. The Spitfire was sleeker ; its designer had taken advantage of more recent knowledge

A HAWKER TEMPEST 5, FAMOUS AS A FIGHTER BOMBER.

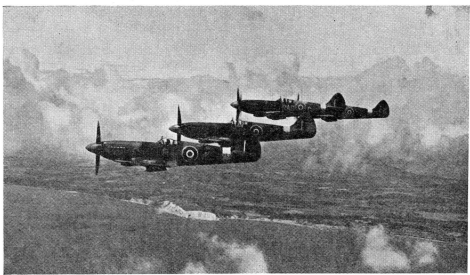

By courtesy of] ["*Flight.*"
SPITFIRES OF A ROYAL AUXILIARY AIR FORCE SQUADRON IN FORMATION.

in airframe construction. The Spitfire was faster and was well suited to the task in which it later distinguished itself—the interception of enemy fighters—leaving the Hurricane to play havoc with the invading bombers.

Thus, for the Battle of Britain, these two fighters were a perfectly balanced team, with Hurricanes outnumbering Spitfires by about two to one, and both being outnumbered by the enemy by something like ten to one. How grateful the country was that her aeronautical engineers were so bountifully blessed with genius, that her Air Force chiefs had had the vision to foster the eight-gun fighter—no fighter had previously had more than four guns—and that her pilots could back their courage with skill and exploit their skill with superb weapons.

The Hurricane remained in production and in service almost to the end of the war. The Spitfire neither went out of production nor out of service during that time; its classic silhouette was still a familiar sight in many skies for years after hostilities had ended.

A Formidable Night Fighter

When the Luftwaffe sought the safety of darkness and opened the Battle of the Night Skies its casualties were light. Eight months later its losses were so heavy that night bombing had become unprofitable. In May, 1941, England had its last heavy raid of the war. Later raids, though sometimes sustained over considerable periods, lacked the weight and fury of that first desperate bid to knock England out from the air as the alternative to invasion.

In those eight months to May, 1941, the Royal Air Force brought to a high state of efficiency a new system of night interception—a system in which radar was carried into the air for the first time. It was installed in a new night fighter, the Beaufighter. Ground radar and radio telephony guided the interceptor to the vicinity of the raider. When the fighter's radar picked up the enemy the chase was on with a vengeance, and lucky indeed was the bomber that got away. The Beaufighter could open up with four 20-mm. guns and six ·303-in. machine-guns, and literally blast the enemy out of the sky.

The Beaufighter won its spurs in the Battle of the Night Skies, but added new lustre to its fame in many other roles as the war spread to fresh skies. It proved to be a competent " ground-strafer," and when it went to the Far East theatre of war the Japanese, amazed by its silent approach and shattering blows, called it "Whispering Death." It became fighter-bomber, torpedo carrier and rocket-projectile aircraft and left

[*Charles E. Brown.*
SAUNDERS-ROE S.R.A/I JET-PROPELLED FLYING-BOAT FIGHTER.

62

[Crown Copyright Reserved.

A SIKORSKY HELICOPTER IN SERVICE WITH THE R.A.F.

trails of havoc every time it went on "ops." It was one of the
R.A.F.'s finest weapons of World War II and has every right to
appear with the Hurricane and Spitfire on the scroll of fame.

The next warplane to come into the limelight fulfilled so many
functions that no single category can encompass them. It began life
as an unarmed bomber. Never before had anyone proposed anything so revolutionary ; even the Air Ministry doubted the worth of
a bomber which relied for success and defence upon sheer speed,
and they guarded against failure by asking that the company should
also build a similar bomber with guns.

The gunless bomber was built first, and tested. Its astonishing
speed and manœuvrability banished the Air Ministry's doubts and
the armed version was never finished. Within a few months the
enemy was being attacked by a venomous, insect-like bomber which
darted here and there and dropped its bombs—sometimes 4,000-
pounders—in the least expected places. How well named they must
have thought it—this Mosquito !

There were few jobs the Mosquito could not do. It became a

63

fighter armed with four 20-mm. cannon and four ·303-in. machine-guns, a fighter-bomber with a 2,000-lb. bomb-load, a fighter-bomber with bombs and rockets, an unarmed photographic reconnaissance aircraft, and one version had a six-pounder anti-tank gun—a veritable piece of artillery—installed in its slim but capacious fuselage, for attacks on submarines. In all, more than forty different versions of the British-built Mosquito were made—and Canada and Australia added further versions to the list.

By courtesy of]   [*The " Aeroplane."*

AN AGILE BIPLANE.

Gloster Gladiator starting a loop. These machines touched the peak of manœuvrability before the coming of the faster but less agile monoplanes.

That strange period of quiet which followed the declaration of war by Great Britain, France and the Commonwealth countries—called, at that time, the " phoney war "—was broken only at sea and by intermittent air attacks on naval targets. Neither the Germans nor the Allies seemed anxious to unleash the full fury of all-out air attack on cities. As a result, an odd duty befell the R.A.F.'s bomber squadrons.

They used to set off, usually from home bases, to drop thousands of pamphlets on German towns warning the people of the folly

By courtesy of]

[Messrs. A. V. Roe & Co., Ltd.

THE ROCK AND AIRSTRIP OF GIBRALTAR SERVE AS THE BACKGROUND OF THIS COLOURED
DRAWING OF THE AVRO SHACKLETON RECONNAISSANCE BOMBER.

By courtesy of] [Vickers-Armstrongs, Ltd.
VALETTA MILITARY TRANSPORT WITH PARATROOPER AT DOOR READY TO DROP.

into which they had been led by their Führer. The parcels of printed propaganda were called " bomphlets " and the bombers which distributed them were the Hampden, the Wellington and the Whitley —chiefly the Whitley.

All three were twin-engined monoplanes and were then the R.A.F.'s heavy bombers. But the moment Germany invaded Norway in the spring of 1940, the bombers loaded more war-like cargoes, and ceased to be " bomphleteers."

Their replacements had been planned as far back as 1936, but changes had to be made in the planning of two of them. Only the first, the Stirling, had begun its flying tests before the war ; the others, the Manchester and the Halifax, appeared later. Then the Manchester had to be withdrawn because the engine around which it had been designed was taken out of production. In its place came the Lancaster.

The Stirling, the Halifax and the Lancaster were four-engined ; the Manchester was a twin. All could carry big bombs great distances ; the Lancaster topped them all by lifting the gigantic 22,000-pounders which had been specially designed to deal with targets of exceptional toughness. It was the only bomber of its time that could carry a bomb of that size and weight.

The magnitude of the bombing effort into which these bombers, and the Mosquito, were thrown can be judged by the fact that, in 1944 alone, Bomber Command dropped more than 525,000 tons of bombs. The greatest weight of bombs dropped in any one night of the war was just under 5,500 tons, and the greatest weight dropped in twenty-four hours was 10,300 tons. This indicates the intensity of the offensive. Often the number of bombers despatched exceeded a thousand, and once or twice reached 1,400.

Whitleys and Hampdens were gradually withdrawn from Bomber squadrons as the new types came along, but the Wellington remained in service throughout the war, and was still in use as an advanced trainer for years after the war's end. Something like 10,000 were built before production ended.

Space must be found for mention of a fighter that ought never to have had a war record—the Gladiator, a biplane fighter which was caught up in the war just as it was on the point of retiring from active service. But of all the Gladiators which went into battle, the most famous are " Faith," " Hope," and " Charity "—three naval Gladiators which, found in crates on a Malta quayside, were unpacked, assembled, fuelled and flown against the Regia Aeronautica —the Italian Air Force. Their success re-kindled the flame of hope that Malta might be held though it stood on the very doorstep of Italy. The defences were manned again, and a famous epic was enacted.

In glowing words, history tells of Malta's terrible ordeal under the double assault of the Luftwaffe and Regia Aeronautica ; of the gallantry of the defenders, of the restoration of the island's strategic importance and its final and well-deserved honour—the award of the George Cross. But for those three Sea Gladiators, and the fantastically illogical decision to hurl them against a powerful air force, Malta might have been left to its fate and a vital base thrown away. For this reason, the veteran Gladiator flies side by side in the history of the Royal Air Force with the Hurricane and Spitfire, saviours of the British Isles and, later, defenders of Malta, too.

DE HAVILLAND VAMPIRE.
Designed for high-altitude fighting and one of the R.A.F.'s standard warplanes.

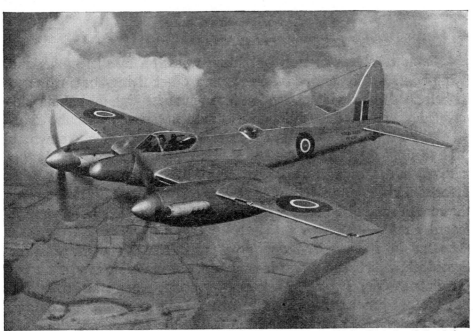

By courtesy of]   [de Havilland Aircraft Co., Ltd.
THE SEA HORNET.
With the radiators of its liquid-cooled engines built into the leading edges of the wings, the Sea Hornet (and its R.A.F. version, the Hornet) was one of the " cleanest " twin piston-engined fighters ever built.

By courtesy of] A GLOSTER METEOR IV. [*" The Aeroplane."*

Fame of a less spectacular nature was won by the Sunderland flying-boat, which, until landplanes and other flying-boats came to its help, had to provide protection for convoys sailing the submarine-infested waters of the Atlantic. It could not watch over the ships all the time they were at sea; there was a large area, known as " The Gap," which no shore-based aircraft could reach, and it was here that the Germans took such heavy toll of our merchant ships before hurriedly contrived aircraft carriers were able to accompany the convoys and give them air cover—the defence which the submarine feared most.

One of the carrier-borne types used for this work was the Swordfish, which had a war history more remarkable even than the Gladiator. The Swordfish was still in service when war broke out, but the last pre-war Swordfish had been built many months before. Its successor had been chosen, but under the test of war disclosed shortcomings that took it out of service. The tried and trusted Swordfish came into its own again; its production was resumed and it went on to win some of the brightest honours of the war in some of the most daring actions known to naval history. Twice Swordfish brought disaster upon the Italian fleet in the Mediterranean Sea ; a Swordfish hit and crippled the fast and powerful German battleship *Bismark*, and sealed its fate ; Swordfish were constantly on the hunt for enemy merchant shipping. They were part and parcel of the Royal Navy afloat and ashore, and there are thousands of naval airmen who remember with deep affection the clumsy-looking biplane officially called " Swordfish " but to them—just " Stringbag."

A score or more other aeroplanes deserve mention for the large and small parts they played in the bitter struggle for victory. The Battle, Defiant, Blenheim, Lysander, Skua, Fulmar, Beaufort, Anson at the beginning of the war ; the Whirlwind, Tempest, Typhoon, Meteor jet fighter, the Barracuda and the Firefly, all of which came on the scene as the months rolled by. Nor must we forget the Auster, the war's least warlike warplane, which went into battle unarmed and often unescorted to gather and send back to base intelligence about the enemy's strength and positions in the battle area, just like those old "spotters" of 1914–18, the "eyes" of the Army.

By courtesy of]   *[de Havilland Aircraft Co., Ltd.*
THE VENOM—A MODERN R.A.F. FIGHTER.

SOME FAMOUS R.A.F. PLANES

The end of the war found a number of new warplanes being groomed for action. There was the four-engined Lincoln bomber, a more powerful version of the Lancaster. There was the long-range, single-seat twin-engined Hornet fighter; the newest version of the Spitfire (named Spiteful); the nippy little Vampire single-seat, single-engined jet fighter; the naval Firebrand and the Spearfish; the aggressive-looking Brigand, and various others. All might have won battle honours against Japan had she not thrown up the fight in August, 1945.

Since then, newer versions of these and earlier types, and others, have made their bow—the Sea Hawk, the Naval Attacker and P.510 and P.1052 jet fighters, the SR/A1 jet flying-boat fighter (the only one of its kind in the world), the Wyvern naval fighter, the Devon, Valetta and Hastings transports, the Canberra high-flying medium jet bomber, the Fairey 17 and Blackburn anti-submarine aircraft. Since then, too, work has started on heavy jet bombers of amazing power and astonishing performance, and with shapes never before seen in the skies; graceful, with engines hidden, unusual lines and novel forms of construction.

These big jet bombers were still secret when this book was written and all the nations were waiting expectantly to see whether Great Britain had, once more, maintained her reputation as the builder of the world's finest warplanes.

A COASTAL COMMAND FLYING-BOAT FLOWN BY THE ROYAL AUSTRALIAN AIR FORCE.

By courtesy of]   [*Hawker Siddeley Group Ltd.*

THE AVRO VULCAN.
The world's first four-jet operational Delta bomber.

A MODERN WARPLANE

WHEN aeroplanes were first put to military use they could be kept in good working order by a motor mechanic, a sailmaker and a carpenter. (The sailmaker looked after the fabric covering.) Now, warplanes need the expert attention of highly skilled engineers whose training takes two to three years and costs the country hundreds of pounds. The skilled men have assistants who have also had to be trained in their duties and, like their colleagues, proved efficient by examination.

To outward view, the modern warplane gives little indication of its structural complexity or of the multiplicity and diversity of its equipment. But step inside a bomber, or glance into the cockpit of a fighter, and the scene that meets the eye removes any doubt. There are instruments, switches, levers, knobs, handles, controls, lamps, meters, warning devices, gauges, fire extinguishers, oxygen bottles, plugs, release pins and radio apparatus filling almost every nook and cranny, till it seems that no room remains for the crew. Then remember that the crew are often dressed in thick warm clothing and you realize how the increasing " mechanization " of the aeroplane has put a premium on space and taxed the ingenuity of the designer. There is hardly anything that the crew must do manually —beyond pressing a button, or moving a lever or switch. At their command is power unlimited, and the muscular effort normally needed to fly the biggest bomber could be furnished by the average healthy, well-developed youngster.

But the scene that greets the eye in a warplane ready for an operational flight is neat and orderly compared with that when it is being overhauled. Take out the dashboard in front of the pilot and you will see an assortment of wires and pipes which, to the untrained eye, makes a picture of complete confusion. How dismayed a motor mechanic would be at the mere sight of it ! Yet the men who keep these warplanes flying know the purpose and function of every wire and every pipe, every chain and cable, every screw and washer.

A big bomber at rest on the ground is an inanimate object, but in flight it is a living creature with a muscular and nervous system not unlike that of the human body. The brain that

[*By courtesy of Gloster Aircraft Co., Ltd.*

This cut-away drawing shows some of the internal structure of a Meteor 8 twin-jet fighter.

By courtesy of]   [*Armstrong Whitworth Aircraft Ltd.*

METEOR N.F.11 NIGHT FIGHTER.

Designed by the Gloster Aircraft Co., Ltd., and Sir W. G. Armstrong Whitworth Aircraft Ltd. It is fitted with two Rolls-Royce Derwent 8 engines.

controls the system is the flight deck; it is from here that the commands flash to every point of the complex assembly and cause those essential movements that enable the bomber to taxi out, take off, climb to a great height, follow the correct course, attack its target, defend itself and return to base.

Once an aeroplane is airborne special importance attaches to the control surfaces. Many other parts can go " unserviceable " without bringing disaster, but if the control surfaces fail to function correctly, the aeroplane's safety is immediately imperilled. The failure of almost any other part must be followed by a further hazard before danger of the same magnitude threatens. A useless gun turret, for instance, is no danger until the aeroplane is attacked. Even the failure of one or more engines does not always bring about catastrophe, though it is a dangerous circumstance and often justifies the crew in taking to their parachutes—particularly at night.

The control surfaces consist of the ailerons, the elevator(s), rudder(s) and flaps. The ailerons are long, narrow surfaces hinged to the trailing-edge of the wings near the tips. The rudder is a hinged surface attached to the fin, and the elevator a hinged surface attached to the tailplane.

Flaps may take one of several forms. They may be hinged and simply drop down : only the lower half may be hinged : some are so designed that when they are lowered a slot, or gap, appears between them and the wing : sometimes they are " double slotted " : sometimes they take the form of a small wing which, when not in use, is hidden inside the big wing. Or the flaps may be a separate wing permanently exposed, but capable of being moved up and down.

To bring these surfaces into use the pilot is provided with a control column and rudder pedals (or a rudder bar) and a flap lever or other device for adjusting the flaps. The control column (or " stick," as it is commonly called) is connected by rods, cables and chains to both ailerons and elevators. On large aeroplanes it usually consists of a robust but light column which the pilot can push forward and pull backward. Mounted at the head of the column is another fitting, which may look like a motor-car steering-wheel with a piece removed, or a pair of bicycle handlebars the wrong way round. The backward and forward movement of the column raises and lowers the elevators ; left and right movements of the steering-wheel (or handlebars) raise and lower the ailerons. Pushing the left rudder pedal forward puts on left rudder ; a forward movement of the right pedal puts on right rudder.

The job of the ailerons is to tilt or bank the wings, and for this purpose they work in opposition ; that is, when one goes up the other drops down. The airstream is thus able to exert opposite forces and to bring one wing up and the other down under equal pressure. The job of the elevator is to lift or lower the nose, that of the rudder to turn the nose to left or right. Flaps create more " lift " and more " drag " and they are used in different ways for different purposes.

Some aeroplanes are so big and so fast that the physical stamina of the pilot is barely enough to keep fatigue at bay on a long flight. To help him, power-operated controls are sometimes fitted, the energy which causes the control surfaces to move being derived from some power source. This mechanism is very complicated : it must work instantly, yet without violence : it must be light, yet robust. It therefore needs the hand of an expert to keep it in order or it will always be giving trouble. However, it is not yet widely in use.

Before power-operated controls came on the scene, some of the tedium and fatigue of flying was taken away by the automatic pilot. This (a standard device on all large aeroplanes to-day) holds the aeroplane to a pre-set course, and when its controls are adjusted,

[*Central Press Photo.*

ASSEMBLING AN R.A.F. CANBERRA JET BOMBER.

can turn the aeroplane on to a new course. Cases have been known in which pilots have actually landed their aeroplanes by manipulating the automatic pilot's controls. Landings have also been made, through the automatic pilot, by radio signals from the ground, without any help from the pilot, and with the ground controller watching the aeroplane on the radar screen of a ground-controlled approach system. The automatic pilot's main parts consist of fast-running gyros which, noting any change in the aeroplane's attitude, send signals which are translated into control movements to correct the changes. Like most other instruments in an aeroplane, the automatic pilot is very sensitive and needs skilful care if it is to function properly.

Instruments : The pilot and, where they are carried, the flight engineer, navigator, bomb-aimer and radio operator all need instruments. The number of instruments varies with the size and function of the aeroplane, but there are certain " basic " instruments which are found in nearly all aeroplanes, big and small. These are the

KEY TO FIG. 1 (INSTRUMENT PANEL).

1. Auto pilot pitching control; 2. Pilot's call light; 3. Downward identification light switch; 4. Brakes control lever; 5. "Press to transmit" pushbutton; 6. Camera warning light; 7. Bomb-aiming warning light; 8. Engine speed indicators (4); 9. Boost gauges (4); 10. Auto pilot control switch; 11. D.R. Compass repeater; 12. Ignition switches (4 pairs); 13. Supercharger controls; 14. Slow-running cut-out switches (4); 15. Engine starting pushbuttons (4); 16. Engine booster-coil pushbuttons (4); 17. Engine priming pushbuttons (4); 18. Vacuum gauge; 19. Vacuum change-over cock; 20. IFF master switch; 21. Identification lamps switchbox; 22. IFF demolition switches; 23. Fire extinguishers pushbuttons (4); 24. Air-intake heat control switch; 25. Air-cleaner control switch; 26. Starboard engines fuel cocks (2); 27. Oil pressure gauges (4); 28. Flaps indicator; 29. Port engines fuel cocks (2); 30. Glider tow tail-lamp switch; 31. Emergency light switch 32. External lamps warning light and switch.

chief engine and navigational instruments and they are usually grouped close together in a single "panel."

Among the commoner engine controls are the temperature thermometer, radiator thermometer (on liquid-cooled engines), oil pressure gauge and the engine speed indicator. Flying instruments include the turn indicator, direction indicator, altimeter, airspeed indicator, artificial horizon, climb indicator, air temperature gauge, vacuum gauge and compass.

All these instruments must be very sensitive in their movement, yet because they have to work in low temperatures their bearings cannot be lubricated. (The oil might freeze and the instrument be made useless.) All piston-engined aeroplanes are subject to a great deal of vibration and, although an instrument may be mounted on rubber or springs, some vibration will be felt. Hence, the working parts, fine and delicate as they are, must (particularly on piston-engined aeroplanes) be robust enough to withstand hours of ceaseless joggling.

The men of the Royal Air Force whose duty it is to look after the instruments are some of the most highly trained in the Service. They spend years learning not merely the construction and operation of instruments but the nature of the metals from which the instruments are made, the effects of height and the common causes of defects. This training pays handsome dividends; without the needles and other indicators to supply him with information, the pilot (and the navigator and the flight engineer) is without the means of discovering certain facts which are essential to the safe and accurate

COCKPIT — PORT SIDE

KEY TO FIG. 2 (COCKPIT—PORT SIDE).

33. Portable oxygen stowage; 34. Bomb doors control; 35. Pilot's oxygen connection; 36. Sutton harness release lever; 37. IFF distress switch; 38. Isolation switch for navigator's telephone; 39. Auto pilot controls cock; 40. Auto pilot clutch lever; 41. Undercarriage position indicator; 42. Boost cut-out control; 43. Air supply and brakes pressure gauge; 44. Navigation light switch; 45. Landing lamps switch; 46. Throttle control levers (4); 47. Throttle friction damper; 48. Propeller friction damper; 49. Propeller control levers (4); 50. Auto pilot pressure gauge; 51. Windscreen de-icing pump; 52. Glider tow release; 53. Flaps selector control; 54. Aileron trimming tabs control; 55. Rudder trimming tabs control; 56. Elevator trimming tabs control; 57. Undercarriage control safety bolt; 58. Undercarriage control lever.

FIG. 3

COCKPIT — STARBOARD SIDE

FIG. 3

KEY TO FIG. 3 (COCKPIT—STARBOARD SIDE).

59. Fuel pressure warning lights (4) ; 60. Feathering pushbuttons and fire warning lights (4) ; 61. Pressure head heater switch ; 62. Pressure head test pushbutton ; 63. Oxygen regulator ; 64. Bomb jettison handle ; 65. Engine priming master switch ; 66. Bomb containers jettison switch ; 67. Test ammeter ; 68. Radiator shutter switches (4) ; 69. Flight engineer's oxygen connection ; 70. Fuel contents gauges ; 71. Undercarriage and flaps emergency control ; 72. Flight engineer's seat ; 73. Coolant temperature gauges (4) ; 74. Oil temperature gauges (4) ; 75. Gallons-gone fuel flow-meters (2) ; 76. Booster pump test pushbuttons (4) ; 77. Booster pump switches (4).

flying of the aeroplane. The human senses are sadly inefficient when asked for the information supplied by the instruments. Tests have proved that they not only mislead, but can send signals to the brain indicating conditions which are the very reverse of those prevailing.

As an example : during, and for some years after, World War I (before the range of instruments was as complete as it is now) pilots would often go into a spin, recover, then go into another spin in the same direction as before. Finally, the discovery was made that the pilot, on recovering from the first spin, imagined himself to be spinning in the opposite direction and, thinking to correct this spin, made control movements which put him back into the original spin. During their memorable non-stop transatlantic flight in 1919—the first ever made—Alcock and Brown lost the use of the airspeed indicator while in cloud, and their aeroplane went into a spin. The pilot was unable to stop the spin until he came out of the cloud and had some fixed point on which to focus his eye and base his control movements.

The photographs of the Lincoln's cockpit, reproduced on pages 77 and 78, give a striking illustration of the degree of " instrumentation " in a large piston-engined bomber. These pictures show no fewer than seventy-seven different items, and a close study reveals that many of them are duplicated and still more quadruplicated, making a total of nearly two hundred. An elementary trainer, by contrast, has a comparatively simple cockpit layout, with only the essential engine and navigation instruments for the pupil to master.

The Lincoln and other big aeroplanes have an electrical system that could supply the needs of a large house. On the Lincoln each of the four engines drives a generator. These generators send electricity direct to various parts of the aeroplane and also charge four accumulators. The power generated is used for scores of different purposes : such as starting the engines and feathering the

[*Central Press.*

A HALF-COMPLETED CANBERRA JET BOMBER.

propellers, setting the fire extinguishers off; for altering the setting of the hot-and-cold air control, the air-cleaner control and radiator flap controls; for indicating the amount of fuel consumed; for giving warning of a drop in fuel and oil pressure; for priming the engines, changing the supercharger gear, indicating the amount of fuel in the tanks, the position of the undercarriage, the speed of the engines, working the fuel pumps; for all internal and external lighting, operating the gun turrets, the wing flap indicators, the dinghy release, warming the pressure head of the airspeed indicator to prevent it from icing up; to work the windscreen wiper; for fusing and releasing bombs, transmitting the indications of the D.R. compass, operating the bomb sights, the automatic pilot, flare chute; and for the radio and radar equipment.

Sometimes the electrical power works direct, sometimes it sets in motion another kind of energy, such as hydraulic power. An example of the combined use of electrical and hydraulic power is provided by the Lincoln's nose gun turret. An electric motor works a hydraulic pump which builds up the hydraulic pressure to " drive " the gun turret. The mid-upper turret on the other hand, is electrically operated, and the tail turret is hydraulically operated direct from the bomber's hydraulic system. Hydraulic power is used for retracting the main undercarriage, lowering and raising the flaps, opening and closing the bomb doors, and for the fuel jettison mechanism.

On the Lincoln, as on many other bombers, there is also a pneumatic system. The air is compressed by a compressor driven by the starboard inboard engine, and operates the wheel brakes and the radiator shutters. In addition, there is a vacuum system supplied by three suction pumps. Vacuum power is needed for some of the flying instruments, for the bomb sight and computor, and for certain other equipment when carried.

So far, the things listed here form part of the aeroplane and its essential services. Precautions have also to be taken against " emergencies." Thus, we find stowed in convenient places such things as parachutes, air/sea rescue equipment—in the form of dinghies complete with sail, radio, food and drink—portable oxygen bottles, axes, asbestos gloves, first-aid outfit and signalling pistol.

The diversity and complexity of the modern warplane's equipment and fittings are matched by the multiplicity and intricacy of its structure. This is made up of hundreds of small pieces riveted,

[*Crown Copyright Reserved.*

INSTRUCTION IN THE MECHANISM AND WORKING OF A GUN SIGHT AT THE
AIR-GUNNERY SCHOOL.

welded or bolted into one single whole, capable of withstanding the heavy and varying stresses of take-off, flight, manœuvre and landing. The small parts are first joined together to make " sub-assemblies "; sub-assemblies in turn are put together to form sections; and the sections are joined to make the whole.

Take the Lincoln bomber for an example. The wings of this aeroplane have two spars, or girders, as their foundations. Over these run ribs and stringers to give the wings their shape and to provide points of attachment for the metal panels which form their covering.

The wings are made of four sections, excluding the centre section, which forms part of the fuselage, and the tips, which are detachable. Also detachable, and built separately, are the ailerons and flaps.

Inside the wings are six fuel tanks, and among the fittings are balloon barrage cable cutters, a landing light, the port and starboard navigation lights, cables, rods and chains for the movement of the ailerons, mechanisms for raising and lowering the flaps, yards of electric wiring, trimming tabs and balance tabs on the ailerons, and cables for their operation, and bearers for the four engines. These are only a few of the items to be found on or in the wings.

No fewer than five sections make up the fuselage : nose, front centre, intermediate centre, rear centre and rear. The nose section embodies the nose turret and the air bomber's station. The pilot's, second pilot's, navigator's, fighting control and wireless operator's stations are in the front centre section. The intermediate centre section houses sundry items of equipment. The dorsal turret is in the rear centre section, which also contains operational equipment. The rear section carries the tail unit and the tail turret.

The tail unit is made up of four main parts : the fins, rudders, tailplanes and elevators. In general, these are built after the style of the wings with spars and ribs and metal surfaces riveted to the structure. The elevators, like the ailerons, are fitted with trimming and balance tabs. The rudders, too, have trimming tabs but no balance tabs.

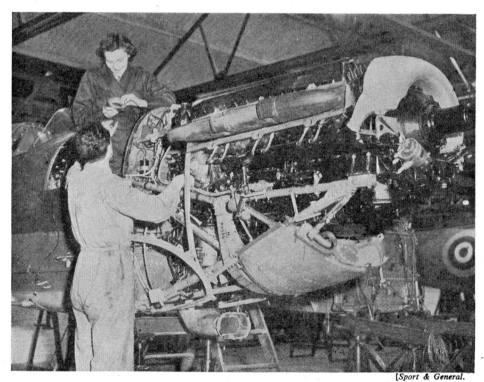

[*Sport & General.*

AN R.A.F. AND A W.R.A.F. FITTER AT WORK ON A PISTON ENGINE.

GLOSTER JET E/38.
The first British jet-propelled aircraft.

[*Crown Copyright Reserved.*

THE MIRACLE OF THE "TURBO" ENGINE

ONE can think of few things more awe-inspiring than the swift silent approach of a jet fighter and its thunderous roar as it hurtles skywards in a rocket-like climb to thousands of feet. There is hardly anything more thrilling than the effortless grace of a jet plane as it rolls, spins, dives and zooms at the command of a skilful pilot. It is always the "jets" that are the stars of the air displays and stay in the memory longest.

Young people take the jet plane as a matter of course, but these fleet-winged craft are apt to leave an older generation gasping with astonishment or lost in admiration. Grown-ups can remember when 60 miles an hour was the world's air speed record, and when a climb to 1,000 ft., which now takes less than six seconds, lasted that number of minutes. The jet engine brought about a sweeping change in aeroplane performance—and it arrived just as the piston engine appeared to be reaching the useful limit of its powers.

The " re-action aero-engine " was foreseen by an eminent French military colonel before the 1914–18 war. The principle of jet

83

By courtesy of]   [Rolls-Royce, Ltd.

Side view of the Nene turbojet as fitted to some of the fastest fighters flying.

propulsion itself is hundreds of years old and its theory had been a favourite topic of discussion among scientists almost from the dawn of history. The Chinese are believed to have been the first to make practical use of it, by means of rockets. Rocket (or jet) propelled missiles were used in many ancient wars, as no doubt your history master told you. But we had to wait for the gas-turbine before we had a really satisfactory form of jet propulsion for aeroplanes.

The gas-turbine had been studied by inventors for more than a hundred years before it was brought to a practical state of usefulness. There must have been scores of attempts by unknown inventors to make a gas-turbine that would work and it was not until the 1930s that anyone could claim success. Most of the pioneering work that ended in success was done in Germany, Switzerland and England, with England and Germany struggling to be the first to make a workable aero-engine. (Gas-turbines can be used for many other jobs besides driving aeroplanes.) Germany won the race, but her lead gave her no great advantage during World War II, and afterwards, defeated and with her aircraft industry disbanded, Germany disappeared as a competitor and England took the lead.

The Royal Air Force has a particular pride in Great Britain's distinction. It was a former R.A.F. aircraft apprentice who, as a cadet at the Royal Air Force College, Cranwell, wrote an essay on the subject of the gas-turbine and later applied his engineering skill to the task of making one work. Supported only by a few friends who shared his faith and hopes, and with only the smallest of

By courtesy of]   [Armstrong Siddeley Motors, Ltd.

The ten stages of the axial-flow compressor (measured against a foot-rule) and the two-stage turbine of the Mamba turbopropeller engine.

resources, he persisted in his efforts until he could show proof that his theories were sound and that a gas-turbine built to his ideas had in it all the elements of success. That was in 1937. The ex-aircraft apprentice is now Air Commodore Sir Frank Whittle, C.B.E., and it was his first primitive-looking engine that provided the foundations for the enormous engineering effort that has since made British gas-turbines famous all over the world and put Great Britain's leadership in this new field of aircraft propulsion beyond doubt. His genius and faith have been recognised by countless scientific and engineering societies of this and many other countries.

By courtesy of] [de Havilland Engine Co., Ltd.
A SIDE VIEW OF THE GHOST TURBOJET ENGINE WITH JET PIPE ATTACHED.

The gas-turbine aero-engine now has a dual personality. It was developed as a turbojet which propelled the aeroplane by creating a small-diameter, high-speed airstream that took the form of a jet. From the turbojet grew the turboprop, which as its name suggests, drives a propeller. The gas-turbine's efficiency lies largely in its simplicity. It has very few working parts ; excluding the accessories which are needed to provide electrical, hydraulic, vacuum and pressurization power, to drive fuel and oil pumps, and (when fitted) a propeller, there is only one main moving part. That is the " rotative assembly," which consists of one or more impellers (or compressors) for compressing the air, one or more turbine wheels, and a plain shaft linking them. Impeller(s) and turbine(s) therefore run at the same speed, with the turbine driving the impeller(s). The turbine gets its energy from the flow of exhaust gases passing through its blades on their way from the combustion chamber to the jet pipe. The turbine blades are short pieces of metal concave on one side, convex on the other, and so arranged around the outer edge of the turbine wheel that they deflect the exhaust gases to one side and as a consequence are themselves deflected in the opposite direction and the wheel thus set spinning.

When we learn that the rotative assembly spins at maximum speeds varying from 7,000 to 15,000 revolutions a minute we realize at once that the exhaust gases must exert tremendous power on the turbine wheel in order to give it such a speed. Our investigations disclose that when the stream of exhaust gases strikes the turbine blades it is travelling at something approaching 1,000 miles an hour.

How is this almost fantastic speed reached ? First, the impeller sucks in huge quantities of air and compresses it so that it is " packed tight," then sends it rushing into the combustion chamber, which consists of a flame tube and an outer casing. Here, some of it is directed into the flame tube, mixed with fuel and ignited. The burning causes the air to expand rapidly and to develop a high temperature. Because more air is continually rushing into the combustion chamber under the power of the impeller it can only expand and move onwards. To make it travel even faster the

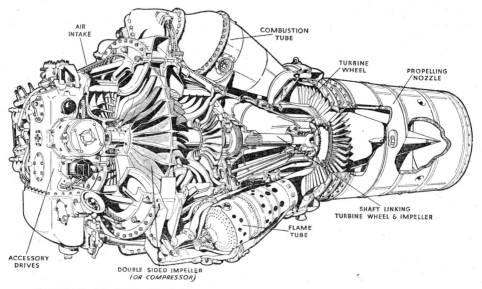

SECTIONAL DRAWING OF NENE TURBOJET SHOWING MAIN STRUCTURAL FEATURES.

THE ARMSTRONG SIDDELEY " SAPPHIRE " TURBOJET ENGINE WHICH USES THE AXIAL-FLOW
SYSTEM OF COMPRESSION AND HAS A SINGLE COMBUSTION CHAMBER.

combustion chamber is narrowed towards the discharge nozzle. The combined influence of the burning and the expansion in the combustion chamber and the narrowing of the escape route compel the gases to " get a move on," and the great spurt which they make is revealed by the fact that in one well-known engine the air flows at approximately 375 miles an hour just before it reaches the turbine wheel, at 800 miles an hour just aft of it, and at more than 1,000 miles an hour from the exhaust nozzle. Any given particle of air which is caught up by the impeller is out in the free air again within a fraction of a second, having been compressed, mixed with fuel, burned, heated and expanded, then hurled out via the jet pipe !

Most of the energy which the exhaust gases give to the turbine wheel is needed to drive the impeller, but enough is left over to send jet planes tearing through the skies at up to 700 miles an hour or more. When the gas-turbine drives a propeller, the surplus energy which goes out as " thrust " in a turbojet is " tapped " by the inclusion of an extra turbine wheel, or perhaps two extra turbine wheels. The energy absorbed by these turbine wheels is transmitted to the propeller either through the rotative assembly or through a freely

By courtesy of]   [de Havilland Engine Co., Ltd.

A "rotative assembly" from a gas-turbine jet engine, showing the turbine wheel and a single-sided centrifugal-type impeller, with the shaft to which both are bolted.

spinning turbine with its shaft running inside that of the rotative assembly.

In both instances, a reduction gear is introduced between the rotative assembly (or between the independent turbine wheel) and the propeller shaft so that the propeller can run slowly enough to be efficient. If spun faster than the speed of sound (which is about 761 miles an hour at sea level at standard temperature) the tips of the blades send out "shock waves" and the blades lose a lot of their efficiency. The air is unable to "step aside" as it does when meeting slower-moving objects, and it becomes tightly compressed. The reduction gear allows the rotative assembly (or independent turbine) to make something like eight or ten revolutions for every revolution of the propeller. (On a geared piston engine, the reduction is usually two revolutions of the crankshaft to one of the propeller, although some engines have a ratio of three to one.)

Gas-turbines swallow vast quantities of air; even one of only 3,000 lb. static thrust needs about 100 tons an hour. The greater part of this air—some five-sixths of it, in fact—is needed for cooling the engine, not for combustion. Hydrocarbon fuels, among them kerosene, the fuel most commonly used for gas-turbines, burn at a temperature of about 2,500° F. A flame of that intensity would soon eat its way through the toughest metal known to metallurgists, so most of the incoming air is allowed to pass round the head (or primary zone) of the flame tube, where combustion begins, and is admitted at intervals

By courtesy of]   [Armstrong Siddeley Motors, Ltd.

A cut-away drawing showing axial-flow compressor and turbine blades of Mamba turbopropeller engine.

through holes in the flame tube walls. This dilution with cold air drops the temperature from 2,500 ° F. to something between 600° and 800° in the region of the turbine wheel. Some of the air is diverted from the main stream to cool the bearings and the turbine wheel and its blades. If this heavy demand for cooling air did not exist the gas-turbine engine could be made much smaller and yet be just as powerful.

For convenience we have made reference to " the combustion chamber " as though a gas-turbine had only one. Some, it is true, have only one, but most of those built so far have had more. One had no fewer than sixteen. Where several combustion chambers are

By courtesy of]   Rolls-Royce Ltd.

ROLLS-ROYCE AVON R A 14 ENGINE. THRUST (WITHOUT RE-HEAT) 9,500 LB.

used they are linked by short tubes through which burning gases can pass. In this way, only one or two combustion chambers need to be fitted with igniter plugs to start the process of combustion ; the rest " borrow a light " from their neighbours through these short tubes. Once combustion starts it is continuous until the fuel supply is shut off.

There are two kinds of impellers. One is known as the centrifugal type, the other as the axial flow. The centrifugal impeller consists of a flat disc on which raised vanes radiate from the centre to the circumference. Sometimes the vanes are on one side of the disc only, sometimes on both. Some gas-turbines (principally turboprops) have two centrifugal impellers (making a two-stage compression system), the second being smaller than the first because the air it has to deal with has already been compressed and reduced in volume by compressor number one. With this system the air is thrown outwards from the centre into several separate combustion chambers. The axial-flow method is quite different. This has rows of short blades set at an angle and mounted on a shaft. As the shaft spins the first row of blades drives the air towards the second, the second to the third, and so on, each row of blades (or each " stage " as it is called) adding something to the degree of compression and to the speed of the air flow. In theory, this system is better than the centrifugal if the air can be kept flowing in a straight line from intake to jet nozzle. However, some gas-turbine engines using the axial-flow system divert the air into a number of separate combustion chambers, so there is no hard and fast rule on this matter.

A further complication occurs when a gas-turbine starts the process of compression with an axial-flow system and rounds it off with a centrifugal impeller ! There are, too, some gas-turbines which have their air intake at the rear, compress the air by driving it towards the front of the engine, then turn it through 180 degrees and force it rearwards down the combustion chamber(s) and out. Perhaps one day the engineers will decide which is the most profitable method of compression, and make it the standard model, but the chances are that some merit will be found in each and that we shall see them all in use for many years to come.

Early gas-turbines were lucky if they could reach a compression ratio of four to one ; nowadays they achieve something of the order of seven to one. This means that by the time it leaves the impeller the air is packed so tightly that it occupies only one-seventh the space it occupied before the impeller got hold of it.

And now a word of warning. Never get near the front of a gas-turbine aero-engine when it is running at full power. More than one mechanic has already been drawn into

A Theseus turbopropeller engine fitted to a Lincoln bomber experimentally.

THE MIRACLE OF THE "TURBO" ENGINE

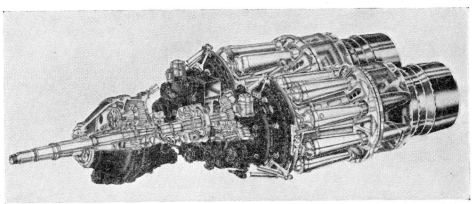

TWO PROTEUS PROPELLER-TURBINE ENGINES COUPLED TO FORM A SINGLE POWER UNIT
DRIVING TWO AIRSCREWS TURNING IN OPPOSITE DIRECTIONS.

the air intake and fatally injured, so powerful is the suction of the impeller. You will hardly need warning never to stand close to a working jet engine in a direct line with the propelling nozzle. You would find things decidedly hot. They would be hotter still if the engine happened to be using "after burning" (or re-heat) equipment. This increases the thrust by burning additional fuel in the jet pipe. The fuel burns with a tremendous roar and can be guaranteed to give you a swift, thorough and free hair-singe—eyebrows and all—if you get too near!

In this discussion we have rather neglected the piston engine; but that does not mean that the piston engine is dead and awaiting burial. Its days may be numbered, but it will be an active partner of the gas-turbine for some years yet.

The piston engine has had a long innings and it seems strange, now, that the gas-turbine arrived almost at the very moment when the engineers were wondering whether it would be worthwhile developing the piston engine any further. Up to 3,500 horse-power the piston engine had a good power-to-weight ratio, but it seemed that with increasing power the weight would increase out of proportion to the gain. This was disputed by some engineers, but the matter was never put to test and is never likely to be. The gas-turbine has too many advantages to leave the piston engine any claims for development beyond outputs already obtainable.

True, it has lower fuel consumption than the gas-turbine judged on an "out-put" basis at sea level, but the gas-turbine's consumption improves the higher it flies, until at very great height and high speed the piston engine's advantage is much reduced. For this reason, any device which enables a turbojet or turboprop-engined aeroplane to climb quickly will find favour. One of the most promising is the rocket engine. Regular rocket-assisted take-offs were first tried during World War II in association with piston-engined warplanes, and experiments with commercial air-liners after the war have shown that rockets add no danger and bestow substantial benefits. They may also be used for high-speed cruising at great height, where ordinary internal combustion engines tend to lose much of their power through lack of oxygen with which to burn the fuel. The rocket scores because it carries its own oxygen, but has a short working life in proportion to the weight of fuel, compared with the piston engine and gas-turbine.

There is the distant prospect that one day aeroplanes may fly on atomic power. One or two experts have dismissed the suggestion as impracticable because, they say, atomic motors will always be exceptionally heavy. But looking back over recent history and noting the number of false prophecies that have been made in many

PUPILS AT AN R.A.F. TECHNICAL SCHOOL WORKING ON A TURBOJET ENGINE.

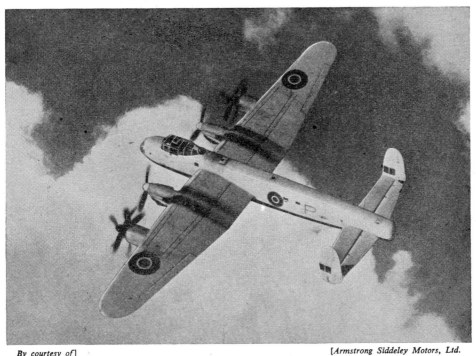

By courtesy of] [Armstrong Siddeley Motors, Ltd.

AN AVRO LANCASTER BOMBER.
With two Python turbopropeller engines and, inboard, two Merlin piston engines.

branches of engineering, only the rashest among us would rule out the atomic aero-engine as impracticable.

Propellers: When it was announced that Great Britain had jet-propelled fighters in the air, the shares of all propeller companies slumped badly. Investors imagined that almost overnight propellers (which are often referred to as "airscrews") had been made obsolete. Instead, they have since grown bigger and still more versatile.

The simple propellers of the kind fitted to elementary trainers are made either of laminations (or layers) of wood glued together, or of metal, formed to the appropriate size and shape. The "pitch" (or twist) of their blades cannot be altered and is of the degree which calculations indicate will give reasonably good results in all conditions of flight, but the best in none. The pitch, in other words, is a compromise, and the propeller never approaches its maximum efficiency.

Variable-pitch propellers can adjust the pitch of their blades to the needs of the moment. For take-off, the pitch is set fine so that the engine can run at its maximum speed and thus deliver maximum power. Each slice of air cut by the blades is very thin and the amount of energy demanded from the engine to cut it is small. As soon as the aeroplane reaches a safe height, the blades are given a coarser setting. This increases the thickness of the slice of air cut by each blade, and throws a heavier task upon the engine. The engine cannot deliver any more power (it is already giving its maximum) and it has no alternative but to slow down. This slowing down has the double advantage of reducing fuel consumption and the rate of engine wear, both of which are disproportionately high when the engine is running at top speed. When the piston-engined aeroplane reaches its operating height a further reduction in speed is made. Turboprop engines, however, are normally run at a speed only slightly below maximum in order to secure the best mileage from the fuel consumed. A piston engine, on the other hand, gives best results when running slowly.

The "variable-pitch" mechanism of the propeller serves as a kind of gear-box. There are no fixed gear ratios and the speed of the propeller's rotation in relation to that of the engine crankshaft is not altered. But the "variable-pitch" propeller can be adjusted to an infinite number of positions between maximum fine and maximum coarse. Many variable-pitch propellers also have a device which, by altering the pitch of the blades, keeps the engine running at a pre-determined speed with no attention from the pilot. This device is called the "constant speed unit" (usually abbreviated c.s.u.); it works on the principle of the governor which controls

By courtesy of]   *[de Havilland Engines, Ltd.*

THE GOBLIN.

Power unit of the Vampire fighter and D.H. 108 experimental and research planes.

By courtesy of]   [*Rolls-Royce Limited.*

This Meteor twin-jet fighter has after-burning (or re-heat) equipment fitted to the jet pipe of its Derwent engines
to enable the pilot to increase the total thrust in an emergency.

the speed of an ordinary clockwork gramophone turntable, and
sends appropriate "commands" to the pitch-changing mechanism
in the propeller hub. If, for instance, the engine increases speed
the c.s.u. sends a signal telling the hub mechanism to coarsen the
pitch of the blades. When the readjustment is made the engine
finds it impossible to keep up its speed because the blades demand
more energy from the engine to spin them and, receiving no extra
fuel to provide the extra energy, the engine slows down. Conversely,
if the engine runs too slowly, the c.s.u. signals for a finer pitch and
the engine, relieved of a little work, "revs up." The c.s.u. thus
saves the pilot from having to correct the inevitable variations in
engine speed that occur on most flights from one cause or another,
and he is able to give more attention to the flying of the aeroplane.

Following the variable-pitch propeller came the "feathering"
propeller. This carries the variable-pitch principle a stage further
and enables the pilot, if an engine fails, to turn the blades "edge on"
to the airstream and bring the "dead" engine to a stop. Without
this facility, the propeller would windmill (or "twiddle"), and
perhaps cause serious damage. Cases have been known where a
windmilling engine has wrenched itself out of the airframe. Further-
more, a windmilling propeller is a prolific source of drag and seriously
reduces the aeroplane's speed at the very moment when speed is
more vital than ever.

After feathering, came reversible-pitch propellers with blades

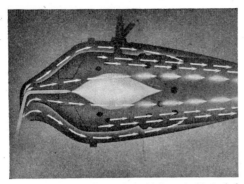

Some air enters the flame tube and is burned with the fuel in the " primary zone," while the rest enters through spaced holes in the flame tube in order to reduce the temperature of the gas.

which can be turned in their sockets until their " thrust " goes forward and they try to push the aeroplane backwards. The first purpose of the reversible-pitch propeller was to assist the manœuvring of large flying-boats on the water. Its primary purpose, now, is to enable land-planes to be slowed down quickly and smoothly on landing, without the use of brakes.

Care has to be taken about the timing of the reversal and normally this does not take place until the aeroplane's wheels are actually on the ground. Then, with blades in reverse pitch, the engines are " opened up " and the aeroplane's forward speed is quickly checked, thus reducing the landing run and saving a great deal of wear and tear on the brakes, wheels and tyres.

Experiments have also been made to test the value of reversible-pitch propellers for bringing aeroplanes down quickly from great heights. Results indicate that very fast, safe descents can be made in this way and it seems likely that, when high flying becomes general, this method of losing height at the end of a journey may become a standard practice.

Blade pitch-changing is usually done by oil, hydraulic or electric power, but there is one

[*Keystone.*

Eight-bladed contra-rotating propeller of Westland Wyvern naval strike fighter.

A VAMPIRE ATTACKING FROM ASTERN.
From a coloured drawing by Wootton.

type of variable-pitch propeller which uses weights and another which is operated manually. The weighted propeller varies its pitch according to the speed of the propeller, and the makers claim that this automatic method ensures that the blades will always take up the correct pitch whatever the need of the particular moment might be.

VICKERS SUPERMARINE TYPE 510 EXPERIMENTAL FIGHTER WITH NENE
TURBOJET ENGINE.

Naturally, a price has to be paid for variable-pitch, feathering and reversing propellers. Their working parts have to be strongly and finely made, they are heavier and need more attention than the fixed-pitch propeller. But they repay a hundred times over their cost, weight, complication and the attention they demand. If the propeller-driven aeroplane had still to rely upon fixed-pitch propellers it would be a very inefficient vehicle. Many, in fact, would never be able to leave the ground without assistance from some other kind of power.

By courtesy of]   [Vickers-Armstrongs, Ltd.

A VARSITY CREW TRAINER AS USED BY THE R.A.F.

THE THREE-SEAT PRENTICE BASIC TRAINER.

THE BADGE OF THE QUALIFIED R.A.F. PILOT. IN OTHER WORDS,
THE COVETED " WINGS."

WINNING
THOSE COVETED WINGS

TWENTY-FIVE years ago an R.A.F. pilot, his tunic newly
decorated with " Wings," could pass from the elementary trainer
to an " operational " warplane with but little further instruction.
The mechanization and instrumentation and technical complication
we have read about had barely begun, and the jump from the simple
school aeroplane to the " deadliest " fighter of the 1920s was a mere
hop.

What a brief career the pupil of to-day would have if he jumped
from his elementary trainer to a 600 miles an hour bomber! His
jump has to be by stages : from elementary trainer to advanced
trainer ; from operational trainer to operational warplane.

For years, experts said that the more elementary the elementary
trainer was the better the trainer it made. The pupil, it was argued,
had enough to think about in trying to grasp the first rules of flying,
and any form of complication which made further demands on his
attention and required further actions from him could not be
admitted. Therefore, the elementary trainer is normally devoid of
most of those technical refinements—such as supercharged engine,
variable-pitch propeller and retractable landing-gear—which tend to

THE INSTRUMENT DASHBOARD OF THE CHIPMUNK BASIC TRAINER.

add to his difficulties and divert him from the basic throttle-stick-and-rudder-bar processes of take-off, flight and landing. There is strong evidence to support this.

Through concentrating too hard on landing, many a pilot has forgotten to lower his undercarriage. As a safeguard, aeroplanes used to be fitted with warning devices—visual and aural—usually in the form of red lights and electric horns. One day, a pilot was seen to be landing with his wheels up. He was called by radio and told that his undercarriage was not down, but he continued his descent and finished up with a belly landing—which didn't do the aeroplane much good. When they asked him why he had ignored the radio call he replied : " I couldn't hear what you were saying ; the undercarriage warning horn was making so much noise."

Another young pilot, who had flown about a dozen different types of aeroplanes, was boasting to his less experienced co-pilot as they circled an airfield : " There isn't much difference between one aeroplane and another, you know ; they're all very much alike." Then, with the skill of a veteran, he made a perfect landing on the concrete runway of an airfield—forgetting that he was piloting a flying-boat !

These lapses are, fortunately, very rare and the average pupil learns his cockpit "drill" thoroughly as he is introduced to the more complicated types. Forgetfulness can carry penalties ranging from humiliation to accident. Even the setting of a trimming tab before take-off is a matter of the gravest import on certain occasions. One very distinguished R.A.F. officer, who piloted his own aeroplane long after he might have had the services of another pilot, was a "stickler" for cockpit drill, and used to insist upon completing every detail—often to the secret annoyance of the ground crew. But he never had an accident, although he would tackle bad weather and other hazards with the next. He was methodical and did not tempt fate by taking an unnecessary chance. He retired from the R.A.F. with a very full log of flying hours and a comfortable pension.

Learning to fly in the Royal Air Force is not one long succession of flying lessons. In fact, more time is spent in the classrooms than in the air. When one is shown the complexity of the modern aeroplane, and understands the many duties in the air and on the ground that fall to an R.A.F. pilot, this is not surprising. Merely being able to fly, we discover, is almost the smallest part of being a pilot!

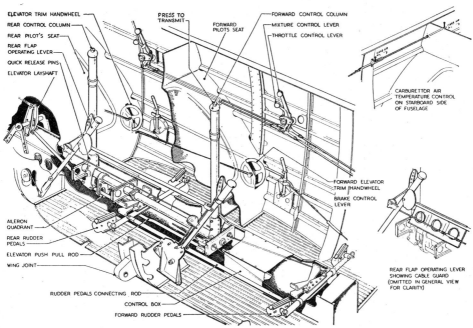

By courtesy of]   [*de Havilland Aircraft Co., Ltd.*

This diagram shows some of the constructional features of the Chipmunk trainer, which is of comparatively simple design.

WINNING THOSE COVETED WINGS

However, a lesson in the classroom can never be as thrilling as a lesson in the boundless sky, so let us turn our backs on blackboards, chalk, notebooks and pens, don flying kit and make sport among the clouds. But wait ! Before we have our first flying lesson let us have " a joy-ride." While there is no serious business on hand we can deliver ourselves up in complete abandon to the thrills and sensations of our first venture into the airman's world. From the ground, our eyes can seldom encompass more than a " few miserable acres " ; from his airborne look-out the airman can view hundreds of square miles in a single glance. So, let's go.

First, there comes the strange illusion that the earth glides slowly away from the aeroplane as we take off ; that it tilts as the aeroplane turns ; that the aeroplane slows down as it gains height until it seems almost stationary.

How fast those straggling clouds flash by ! How " bumpy " it is below this vast unbroken blanket of cloud ! How dense the cloud bank seems ; and what a brilliant scene greets the eye as we suddenly burst through it into sunlit radiance above. Mile upon mile of dazzling cloud-land — mountain, desert and valley stretching to every point

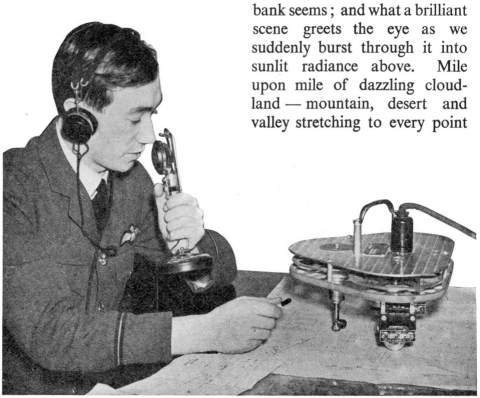

THE ELECTRIC GRAPH RECORDS FOR THE INSTRUCTOR THE PROGRESS OF HIS PUPIL'S FLIGHT.

[*Fox Photos.*

SHOWING THE CHART OR RECORD OF HIS FLIGHT TO THE PILOT.

of the compass, fantastic and unreal ! Far above us, woven into a most intricate pattern, lies a thin film of lacy cloud like a gorgeous veil spread over the whole world. We are lucky ! The heavens do not always deck themselves out like this to delight the air traveller's eye. They have many moods, and may as often imperil as enchant us. To-day, they are staging scenes of grandeur ; how could we have given thought to the opposing action of the ailerons, or the turning effect of the rudder, had we chosen to have a lesson ?

Through gaps now forming in the clouds—and growing bigger —we catch glimpses of the earth far below. There is a railway train, its rolling white plume looking strangely beautiful, and far too big ; there is a cluster of houses round a village green ; a winding river, a dark black road, a golf course with curious yellow scars scattered over it. (They are the sandy bunkers, set to trap unskilful golfers.)

And so we fly, entranced by the cloudscape around us, yet fascinated by the fragments of our everyday world seen through

[*Central Press.*

THREE PRENTICE BASIC TRAINERS WITH THE R.A.F. COLLEGE, CRANWELL, IN THE
BACKGROUND.

the gaps. Vainly we seek a familiar landmark; fruitlessly we try
to identify objects which, surely, neither Man nor Nature made.
Ah! There is our airfield. To our amazement we find that a gap
now stretches over the greater part of the sky and that the clouds
are not more than a grey smudge far away on the horizon. The
heavens have changed their mood again. Let us land before the
mood changes to fog, low cloud or rain, and we have to pit our skill
against the elements.

THE FIRST LESSON

If you were an R.A.F. pupil you would be instructed in the
" theory of flight " before having your first lesson, so that you would
know why the aeroplane behaves as it does in response to the movement of the controls. We will reverse the process and have a lesson
first. Our lesson will differ a lot from that of the R.A.F. pupil pilot,
because we shall have only one and it will cover as much instruction
as the R.A.F. pupil receives in perhaps half a dozen lessons. You
will see the reason later. Back we go to the trainer, and fasten
ourselves in again. We warm up the engine, test the switches, take
off the brakes and taxi out to our starting point.

Permission to take off is soon given; we lower our flaps a

little, turn into wind, open the throttle, gather speed and when the airspeed indicator shows 50 miles an hour (the R.A.F. measures airspeed in knots, by the way) we ease back the stick (correct name " control column," of course) and start to climb. We set the rate of climb by the airspeed indicator and the engine speed indicator and not until we reach a height of 1,000 ft. do we level off, raise the flaps and reduce the speed of the engine, so that we fly at cruising speed.

The control column of this elementary trainer is quite unlike that of the big Lincoln bomber whose cockpit is illustrated on page 77. It is a simple rod pivoting from the floor of the cockpit, and we can push it backwards and forwards, left or right, or towards any point of the cockpit. When it is moved backwards or forwards only the elevator works ; when it is moved sideways only the ailerons respond ; when it is moved backwards or forwards *and* sideways, both elevator and ailerons move. The rudder pedals are much the same as those in the bomber, and work in the same way.

Now put your hand lightly on the control column and your feet lightly on the rudder pedals, and we will attempt a few easy manœuvres.

First, we will climb. Back a little with the stick. Did you feel the movement ? Up goes the nose and down goes the tail, and our rate of climb indicator tells us that we are gaining height at the rate of 500 ft. a minute. At the end of sixty seconds we

[*Keystone.*

AWAITING HIS TURN TO FLY.

[*Fox Photos.*

A HIGH-PERFORMANCE BALLIOL ADVANCED TRAINER.

observe that the altimeter needle confirms the indication of the other instrument by adding 500 to the 1,000 ft. it was previously showing. To " level off," we move the stick forward to its central position, and the rate of climb indicator shows that we are neither climbing nor losing height.

Now for something more ambitious—a gentle turn to the left. Stick over to the left and, at the same time, a slight forward movement with the left foot to apply rudder. Smoothly and evenly the wings begin to tilt ; the left goes down, the right up. At the same time, the nose begins to creep along the horizon to the left. If we keep the stick over to the left our wings will go on tilting until the aeroplane rolls over, so we move the stick back and take off rudder, and the aeroplane goes on turning. To come out of the turn, we move the stick to the right a little, apply a little right rudder, and as the wings start to level up and the nose to stop creeping along the horizon we bring stick and rudder bar back to their neutral positions and once again we are flying straight and level, without having either lost or gained height. Had we wished to turn to the right we should have made similar control movements but in the opposite directions.

When we pulled the stick back to climb we raised the elevator. The airstream found the raised elevator an obstruction and tried to push it back into its neutral position. This it could not do while we kept the stick back; the result was that the airstream, deflected upwards by the raised elevator, forced the tail down. (The same kind of action results, but in a different manner, when the wind—which is also an airstream—strikes the arms of a windmill and sets them turning.)

When the tail goes down the nose goes up because the aeroplane is balanced around its centre of gravity. This is the point of balance similar to that which you get on a see-saw—but differs because it balances in more than one direction. When we turned to the left we not only "banked" our wings, we also turned our nose, thus "pivoting" around the centre of gravity in two ways.

We can add a further complication by making a *climbing* turn

[*Crown Copyright Reserved.*

PUPIL AND INSTRUCTOR.
This basic trainer, no longer used by the R.A.F., has a hood on the rear cockpit under which the pupil may practise blind flying.

to the left. First, stick over to the left, and left rudder—and now a gradual pull back on the stick while it is still over to the left. The wings tilt, the nose swings to the left, and then lifts. The rate of climb indicator shows that we are climbing.

What have we done? We have set three see-saws going by tilting the wings, turning the nose and lifting the nose. Thus, we have an explanation of the statement so often heard, that flying is a three-dimensional affair. Surface travel is two dimensional; you can only move straight ahead or turn left and right whether you are on a plateau or a mountain. In the air you can fly straight and level, turn left or right and climb or dive. And when you remember that you can also fly upside-down you begin to realize how necessary it is that you become expert with stick and rudder bar before you can pass from the flying school into the squadron.

As soon as you have learned the difficult art of " control co-ordination "—that is, moving the control column and rudder bar at the right time, in the right direction in the right degree for the simpler manœuvres—you will start to learn aerobatics. Everyone has to take instruction in aerobatics whether they have the fighter pilot temperament or the less exuberant character of the bomber pilot.

Aerobatics, to some, are sheer exhilaration, and nothing delights

[*Photograph by Cyril Peckham.*

A thrilling and anxious moment as a war-time pupil pilot, watched by his instructor, sets off on his first solo flight in a Tiger Moth trainer.

A FAMOUS R.A.F. BASIC TRAINER—THE TIGER MOTH.

them more than to run through the whole inventory—loop, slow roll, upside-down flying, stall turn, half-roll, half-roll off the top of a loop, zooms and dives. Others find them thrilling enough, but quickly lose their enthusiasm for this kind of " aerial showmanship."

Actually, aerobatics are necessary in a pilot's training because they give the pupil confidence in himself. If he can complete, say, a slow roll without gaining or losing height, and without swerving left or right, he knows that he is master of his aeroplane; and the knowledge is a great comfort to him.

There would be no point in our learning aerobatics on this flight, because we should have but the vaguest notion of what was happening.

But there is one thing we can do with profit. That is to " stall " our aeroplane. A stall can be dangerous; and in a moment you will see why. We are at 1,500 ft. First, we close the throttle gently and without haste. At once the airspeed indicator needle begins to show the drop in speed. Back it slips; 100 miles an hour—95—90—85—80—75 (the nose is beginning to drop a bit so we pull back the stick to raise it)—70—65—60—(back with the stick a little more) 55, 50—now the stick is right back—but it's no good. We feel the aeroplane give a little shudder ! Down drops the nose ! We dive ! But only for a moment ; the speed goes up, the nose lifts. We open the engine throttle and the airspeed indicator needle creeps back to 105 miles an hour—our cruising speed. In the dive we lost nearly 500 ft.

We shall learn all about the stall in the classroom later on. The demonstration in the air proved one important thing ; if we had not had sufficient space in which to recover we should have hit the ground. Our stall was deliberate ; many stalls are accidental. Our stall was made while we were flying straight and level ; some happen while the aeroplane is banking, and these start at a higher speed and are sometimes followed by a spin.

Pupils are taught how to deal with spins. The instructor shows how to start and how to recover from them. We start as though we were about to stall, but just as the aeroplane gives its little shudder we quickly put on rudder in the direction in which we wish to spin. Down goes the nose and the aeroplane rolls over into a spin. After four or five complete turns we ease the stick slightly forward, at the same time taking off rudder. The spin stops, the nose comes up, we move the stick forward still more till it is in its neutral (or central) position and open the throttle.

[Crown Copyright Reserved.

MODEL-MAKING IS A POPULAR PASTIME WITH PUPIL PILOTS.

'There's your destination," says the instructor to the pupil pilot as they set off on a cross-country flight.

In the early days of flying spins were the cause of many accidents. Neither their cause nor their cure was understood until pilots of exceptional courage deliberately put their aeroplanes into a spin, and found out how to stop it. In those days there were no parachutes, and the experimenters took their lives in their hands when they probed this peculiar phenomenon. But their bravery and skill soon found the answer to a baffling problem and saved hundreds of lives.

Now it is time for us to land. The airfield is about a mile ahead of us and a thousand feet below. We partly close the throttle, put the nose down by moving the stick slightly forward, lower our flaps and begin the landing approach. We cast a quick glance now and again at our airspeed indicator and our rate of climb indicator (which also measures our rate of descent) to see that we are not flying too fast or making too rapid a descent. As we skim over the airfield boundary we close the throttle and, losing speed, gradually bring the stick back so that the nose does not drop. Suddenly we feel a slight bump, then a rumble like the sound of distant thunder, and we know that our wheels are running along the ground. We

111

slow down, then taxi back to the school hangar. We have been flying for three-quarters of an hour—and it seemed like five minutes !

We have tasted the thrills and excitements of flying an aeroplane to add to those of flying in an aeroplane. Now we must try to find an equal enthusiasm for the classroom, because it is there that we learn not only the " why and wherefore " of an aeroplane's flight and the mechanics of the engine and propeller but also a great deal about that important quality called " airmanship," about navigation, armament, meteorology, radio, physics, and the many other subjects that make up the training of an R.A.F. pilot. Of these subjects the most important (from our point of view) is aerodynamics. This is the branch of dynamics which deals with " the forces of air or gases in motion, of resistance to the bodies moving in air, and of pressure exerted by air "—according to the dictionary definition. The pilot's training syllabus allots the subject more than 100 hours of classroom study, so you can judge how highly it is rated by the R.A.F.

For our purpose we need only explain that an aeroplane is sustained in the air by an invisible force called " lift," which is derived from a region of low pressure above the wing and a region of high pressure below the wing—both created by the air as it flows over and under the wing in the manner dictated by the shape of the wing, its attitude to the airstream and the speed of the airflow. The speed of the airflow, of course, is set by the speed of the aeroplane rather than by the speed of the wind ; the only effect the wind has upon an aeroplane is to help it to fly faster over the ground or to slow it down. It does not affect the aeroplane's air speed at all. This has to be remembered when we talk about the airstream ; when aeroplanes were very slow it was no uncommon sight on a windy day to see them actually flying backwards ! This meant that they had been caught in a wind greater than their top speed.

The region of low pressure sucks at the upper surface of the wing and, when the aeroplane is flying right way up, tends to pull the wing upwards. The region of high pressure pushes against the under surface of the wing and, when the aeroplane is flying right way up, tends to force the wing upwards.

The pulling (or sucking) and the pushing start as soon as the air begins to flow over the wings ; that is, when the aeroplane starts to move forward. But lift sufficient to make the aeroplane leave the ground must first exceed the weight of the aeroplane, and this may demand an airstream speed of anything from, say, 50 to 100 miles an hour—perhaps more with very fast aeroplanes. Once this minimum speed is reached the aeroplane can take off and fly—and continue to fly, provided that the speed never falls below the minimum. While the aeroplane is flying at or above the minimum

[Keystone.

A PUPIL RECEIVING LAST-MINUTE ADVICE FROM HIS INSTRUCTOR BEFORE THEY
TAKE OFF IN THEIR 600 M.P.H. JET TRAINER.

speed, the air flows over and under the wings in a fairly smooth and steady stream. If it flies too fast, the flow changes and becomes disturbed. If it flies too slowly, a change of quite a different character takes place. This is the change in which we are particularly interested.

During our flying lesson we " stalled " the aeroplane and it began to fall out of the sky. If we could have watched the behaviour of the airstream we should have seen it break up into a thousand

[*Central Press.*

QUALIFIED PILOTS LEARNING THE HYDRAULIC SYSTEM OF THE JET FIGHTERS THEY FLY.

swirling eddies. We should have seen the break-up start at the rear, or trailing, edge of the wing and sweep forward towards the leading edge. With the break-up all the lift from the upper surface of the wing vanished. But we could not watch the behaviour of the airstream, and the only evidence we had that the smooth flow had changed to turbulence was the little shudder which the aeroplane gave just before its nose dropped and the dive began.

A moment or two later, the aeroplane was under full control again. The brief dive caused the speed of the aeroplane to rise above that vital " minimum " ; the airflow became smooth once more and the regions of low and high pressure reappeared and resumed their pulling and pushing. (Oddly enough the pulling is twice as vigorous as the pushing ; which means that the aeroplane is more pulled than pushed into the air !)

Pupils at an R.A.F. flying training school go far deeper into aerodynamics than we have done. They learn a great deal about drag, weight and thrust as well as lift, about the boundary layer, compressibility, and a dozen other things besides, all belonging to this subject. We merely went deep enough to discover why an aeroplane flies and why it stalls. Many accidents have been caused by stalling, and only by knowing the cause and always remembering it can you be sure that you will not find yourself in one which you did not intentionally bring about.

The pupil pilot does not spend all his time studying and flying. That would soon lead to staleness. Every week he spends so many hours in P.T., sports and games, forgetting aerodynamics and stalls, climbing turns and rocket loops, and giving himself up whole-heartedly to the preservation of a first-class physical state, which is a pilot's most precious possession. When an R.A.F. pilot's health goes, his cockpit days are over. If his trouble is serious it means the end of his R.A.F. career.

Learning to be an R.A.F. pilot is not just a matter of flying lessons. A man who can merely take off, perform a few aerobatics and land without mishap would be of little use in an R.A.F. operational squadron. He would almost certainly become a casualty on his first sortie, and most probably get lost the moment he set off on a cross-country flight.

["*New York Times*" *Photo.*

A "SYNTHETIC" TRAINER DESIGNED TO ACCUSTOM PILOTS TO FLYING JET AEROPLANES.

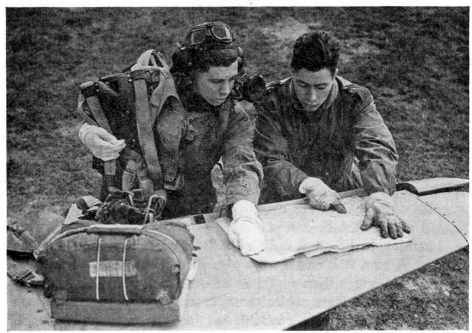

INSTRUCTOR AND PUPIL CHECK THEIR ROUTE BEFORE STARTING A CROSS-COUNTRY
FLIGHT.

FINDING THE WAY IN
THE AIR

FEW things are simpler than getting lost in the air. True, there
are many aids to air navigation, but equally, there are many
impediments, and the navigator (who may also be the pilot) must
have the knowledge and skill to prevent himself from getting lost
and staying lost, or he will become a danger to himself and a menace
to others. The weather is his greatest and most persistent enemy,
seldom his friend.

Air navigation calls for a high standard of intelligence, quick
wits and a well-founded education. The pilot who navigates himself does not go so deeply into the art as the " full-time " navigator, who has his own " station " in the aeroplane, and a bagful of
maps, charts and calculating instruments, and his sextant, to help

116

him to keep track of his position as he flies, or to find it if he gets lost.

The air navigator's course of training in the Royal Air Force is a full and varied one, involving no fewer than 2,500 hours of classroom study and air experience. It teaches him to be familiar with, and know how to use, every one of the many different kinds of maps and charts of his profession, to understand and know how to find and allow for the various errors in the navigation instruments, including the sextant. It takes in the stars, the sun and moon and such subjects as aircraft armament—that is, guns, gun turrets, bombs and bombing, rockets and pyrotechnics—radio, radar, meteorology and those two subjects which we thought (and probably hoped) we had done with when we left school—mathematics and physics. The course also teaches him a good deal about air photography, aero-dynamics, airframes and engines, and explains the different kinds of operational flying upon which he may later be engaged, as well as the purely navigational subjects. In this chapter we can touch only upon one or two of the subjects and then only lightly.

Let us take the navigational flying instruments. They are miracles of precision engineering, but some suffer from defects which are fundamental and cannot be cured. Their errors have therefore to be allowed for by the navigator. The airspeed indicator, for instance, rarely shows the aeroplane's exact airspeed. It is a pressure

By courtesy of]   *[A. V. Roe & Co., Ltd.*
THE NAVIGATOR-PUPIL'S STATION IN AN ANSON T20 TRAINER.
Showing fixed table, radio receiver, altimeter, airspeed indicator, direction-finding loop, visual indicators, repeater compass and clock.

An airspeed indicator calibrated in knots, the standard measurement of speed in the R.A.F.

instrument, and as the air grows thinner and loses pressure with height so the pressure registered by the airspeed indicator falls—with the result that the instrument grows more and more pessimistic until, at 40,000 ft., it is showing only about half the aeroplane's true airspeed. Luckily, we know how much error to allow for at any given height, so that there is little excuse for our being misled by the A.S.I.'s needle.

But the error caused by the drop in pressure with height is not the only error from which the airspeed indicator suffers. There is the position error and attitude error, the first arising from the position of the pitot head through which the pressure is transmitted to the instrument in the cockpit, and the second from the increase and decrease of the Angle of Attack. Both these errors can also be ascertained. (" Pitot," by the way, is pronounced " Peeto.")

The standard altimeter (which works on the principle of the aneroid barometer we use for noting changes in the weather) is also a pressure instrument, but instead of indicating the kind of weather we are about to have, its dial is a scale of measurement, usually in feet. Pressure is not always the same at any given height. For convenience, and by international agreement, a standard measure has been adopted. This assumes (*a*) a sea-level pressure of 1,013·2 millibars, (*b*) a sea-level temperature of plus 15° C., and (*c*) a decrease of temperature with height of about 2° (1·98°, to be exact) for every 1,000 ft. of height. But pressure

A " three-handed " or " sensitive " altimeter, the large hand recording in hundreds, the second in thousands, and the third (smallest) in ten thousands.

118

varies with weather, and a fine spell might give a reading of 1,047 millibars at sea level, while stormy weather might give one of only 911 millibars—a difference of 136 millibars. Therefore, if an aeroplane left a place which was enjoying fine weather and flew to one in the throes of a " deep depression " the aeroplane might find itself at sea level with 3,780 ft. still showing on the altimeter. In bad weather, or at night, that might mean an unpremeditated and violent contact with the ground

[*By courtesy of Henry Hughes & Son, Ltd.*
A MAGNETIC COMPASS.

—in other words, a crash ! Hence, it is customary for the pilot or navigator to make a check, usually towards the end of a long flight, by calling up the base he intends to land at and asking for the local barometric pressure. By means of an adjusting knob he can set his altimeter to agree with the information he receives, and is thus in little danger of being in serious error when it comes to the landing.

Those are two examples of the instrument errors which must be understood and allowed for by pilots and navigators. Even that trusted and proved instrument of navigation, the magnetic compass, is not immune from error. The earth itself is a huge and powerful magnet with its " fields of force " and its North and South ends, like the toy magnets which pick up pins and nails and hold them with the grip of an octopus. The compass has a finely balanced, freely suspended needle which responds to the influence of the earth's magnetic flow, and, unless disturbed, this needle always lies in a north-south direction. The navigator flies by maps based on geographical

An engine speed indicator, or tachometer, with two hands, one registering in hundreds and the other in thousands.

representations, but the North Magnetic Pole, which attracts the compass needle, does not coincide with the Geographic (or True) North Pole. They are, in fact, many miles apart. The angle between the bearings of the Magnetic North and the True North from any point on or above the surface of the earth is called " variation," and it varies from place to place all over the world, and is constantly changing, so that the variation one year at one particular spot is different from that the year before and will be different the year after.

The needle of the magnetic compass is also attracted by *local* magnetic forces which are almost impossible to eliminate from certain types of metal. If the aeroplane were made entirely of wood, or of some metal or material (say plastics) which was free from magnetic influence, this counter-attraction would not occur. But in existing circumstances the counter-attraction exists and the error it causes is known by the name of " deviation."

Counter-magnetization, deliberately brought about, can reduce but seldom correct the combined error arising from variation and deviation, and in order that the pilot or navigator shall know to

COCKPIT OF A DE HAVILLAND MOSQUITO 35 WITH RADAR EQUIPMENT (*on right*).

[*Fox Photos.*

PILOTS ABOUT TO SET OFF ON A FLIGHT BY DEAD RECKONING.
With their instructor they first work out the course.

what extent he must misread the indications of the needle for any particular bearing the aeroplane is placed, in flying attitude—that is, with its tail up and body level—upon a concrete platform known as a compass base, and its compass " swung." The swinging requires that the aeroplane shall be headed, in turn, North, North-East, East, South-East, South, South-West, West and North-West, and that little magnets shall be inserted in the compass to bring the needle as nearly as possible to the point of the compass to which the aeroplane is headed. What error is left is recorded on a card placed near the compass, so that the corrections which are necessary for any given heading can be seen at a glance.

The magnetic compass is often supplemented by a compass which, installed at some point of the aeroplane where local magnetic forces are weakest, transmits its reading to " repeater " compasses in the pilot's cockpit, at the navigator's station, and at other points in the aeroplane. This type is known as the Distant-Reading com-

[*British Official, Crown Copyright.*

TAKING A BEARING WITH A SEXTANT.

pass. Basically, it is a combination of a magnetic compass and a gyroscope, each exerting a measure of influence over the other, and to some extent correcting or modifying each other's more serious defects. For instance, the magnetic compass is too uncertain to be used for accurate turns because it is, among other things, affected by acceleration and deceleration, and the needle also takes too long to settle down again after a change of direction.

By courtesy of Henry Hughes & Son, Ltd.

A PERISCOPIC SEXTANT.

The gyroscope suffers from a process known as " wander "—or drift—and although it accurately registers a turn, it has to be adjusted every few minutes or it will " lie abominably." With the D.R. compass, the gyroscope gives the magnetic compass's needle a measure of stability and the needle keeps a curb on the gyroscope's tendency to wander. Thus, the good qualities of both are brought out and the effects of their shortcomings moderated.

However, the simple magnetic compass remains indispensable because the gyroscope is electrically driven and the source of power may fail. On most flights the magnetic compass is simply a passenger, but it is there if it is wanted.

122

FINDING THE WAY IN THE AIR

In air navigation, compass directions are measured to the nearest degree, clockwise from North—that is, from 000° to 360°—and are always expressed as three-figure groups. Thus, East, which is 90 degrees from North, is written " 090° " ; South is 180°, and West 270°.

Frequent use is made of the term " bearing " in navigation. Any two objects separated by distance have a " bearing " one to another. The bearing is measured clockwise from North and may be expressed as a True (or Geographical), Magnetic or Compass bearing. By taking a bearing on an object whose position is known, a navigator can make a " position line " on his map. He knows only that he is somewhere along that line, but if he can take another bearing on another object whose position he knows and make another position line (which will intersect the first) he has a more precise indication of his whereabouts. If he can find a third object and make a third position line he will have enough information to tell him his position with still greater accuracy.

NAVIGATION PRACTICE IN THE CABIN OF AN ANSON.

[*Fox Photos.*

YOUNG PILOTS RECEIVING INSTRUCTION IN MAP READING.

MAP READING AND DEAD RECKONING

The simplest form of air navigation practised by the Royal
Air Force is map reading. The novice begins by using maps having
enough detail to make identification of landmarks and points of
reference fairly easy, then, by progressive stages, advances to maps
that give only the main topographical details. There are maps for
all purposes ; some have a scale that makes three inches represent
one mile, while on others one inch may represent 32 miles. On
a long flight, a navigator may need a veritable " library " of maps
and charts. If he has to find and identify one small point in the
course of the flight—say a factory, dam or power station—he may
be supplied with a map that shows every house, tree and lane in and
around the spot, but reach the locality by using a map on which
one unit represents two million on the ground—in other words,
the 32 miles to the inch map.

Map reading for a flight begins before the engines are started.
The pilot or navigator first marks his intended route on the map

with a pencil line. He may then mark off the miles as an additional precaution ; if he is a stranger to the route he will certainly make a note of the more prominent landmarks he will see—such as villages, woods, rivers, main roads, golf courses, lakes, large and conspicuous buildings standing in their own grounds—and a note, too, of the approximate time they should come into view. He will also look for prohibited areas on his map so that he can avoid them. They are still fairly numerous, even in Great Britain.

At first, map reading calls for intense concentration. Some of the commonest objects of our everyday world look strange to the airman, and the miles will sometimes slip by while the untrained map reader is deciding what this or that odd thing can be. But practice makes perfect, and the knack of translating the scene below into the pattern of the map, and vice versa, is soon acquired. Those who are already familiar with map reading from rambling, cycling or motoring are, naturally, less handicapped when it comes to map reading in the air.

A SIGNALLER PASSES A MESSAGE TO THE PILOT.

FINDING THE WAY IN THE AIR

Map reading as a form of air navigation has its limitations, and can be used only when the weather offers a reasonably good view of the ground. If clouds are low, or mist or fog obscures the scene, map reading becomes more difficult and less reliable as a means of navigation. It is therefore no good for military operations, which must go on in all but " impossible " weather. From map reading the student therefore passes to navigation by Dead Reckoning, and increases his knowledge, skill and usefulness.

In spite of its name, this form of navigation is very much alive. As a matter of fact, " dead " is a corruption of the first syllable of " deduced," a word which more or less explains that there is an element of uncertainty about it. All R.A.F. aircrew who navigate must be competent dead reckoners. Dead reckoning makes them independent of most of the navigational aids, such as radio and radar, which might not for one reason or another be available, or if available might be unreliable. (We used to mislead German bombers by " bending " the radio beam along which they flew, and make them miss their target.) " D.R." is not a precise form of navigation, but those skilled in its use can rely upon being no more than 20 miles " out " at the end of a 200-mile flight, even though the ground has been out of sight all the way. Normally, the pilot or navigator is able to identify his whereabouts by means of a map when he nears his destination.

Dead reckoning is the art of calculating the course, track, ground speed and position of an aeroplane in flight from knowledge of the probable wind velocity and true air speed. Unless the wind is dead ahead or dead astern, it will always blow the aeroplane off its course, and the track over the ground will be something like the track of a boat crossing a fast-flowing river. The boat is " aimed " at a point well upstream from the intended landing place, and the boatman will row, or the helmsman steer, with an apparent intention of reaching the point aimed at. But the stream causes the boat to drift and the boat will actually arrive at the intended landing place, having been carried there by the stream. Navigation by dead reckoning requires that the navigator shall, before setting off, estimate, by calculation, the extent to and direction in which he must " aim off " in order to arrive at his intended destination.

He therefore consults his map to find the bearing of his destination from his point of departure, then the weather report to find

FINDING THE WAY IN THE AIR

AN R.A.F. " MET." OFFICIAL TELLING AIRCREWS WHAT KIND OF WEATHER THEY MAY EXPECT
DURING THEIR NIGHT FLYING EXERCISES.

out the speed and direction—that is, the velocity—of the wind. He
finds out the amount of compass error he must allow for, and finally
arrives at the magnetic course which he must steer. He has ways
and means of finding out if the wind changes its direction or speed,
or both, while he is flying, and instruments which simplify any
calculations which become necessary in applying corrections to the
original course which he worked out before starting.

In the brave old pioneering days, lone pilots used to set off from
England to fly to India, Australia, New Zealand, South Africa and
even to America—across featureless wastes of deserts and oceans
—using only dead reckoning methods, and seldom got lost. They
had no radio on which to call up for a position " fix " ; they had,
instead, a high degree of navigation skill and—still more important—
an infinite capacity for taking pains in their reckonings. That is
what saw them safely through.

Thus, dead reckoning can be described as the cornerstone of
air navigation, in spite of the many and wonderful aids the navigator
and navigating pilot can call upon in the ordinary course of flying,
both in peace and in war.

FINDING THE WAY IN THE AIR

ASTRONOMICAL NAVIGATION

On very long journeys, it is the custom of the navigator to find or check position by sighting his sextant upon some astral, or heavenly, body, such as the sun, moon or stars. Making use of these heavenly bodies is known as astronomical navigation, and the higher the aeroplane flies the better are the navigator's chances of

[*Crown Copyright Reserved.*
THE NAVIGATOR OF AN R.A.F. FLYING-BOAT PLOTS HIS COURSE.

being able to practise it. Seldom do clouds extend much above 20,000 ft.

When the sky is clear, and there is no moon, the heavens teem with stars; they are beyond counting. But of all those thousands upon thousands of stars, the navigator need be familiar only with about twenty-four, although there are another thirteen which he should be acquainted with. For navigation purposes, the stars are numbered as well as named, and the longer names are usually abbreviated.

By courtesy of]   *[The Gloster Aircraft Co., Ltd.*

GLOSTER METEOR JET-FIGHTER TAKING-OFF.

From a coloured drawing by R. S. Franklin.

FINDING THE WAY IN THE AIR

Most important star of them all, in the Northern Hemisphere, is Polaris, the Pole Star (No. 47). This indicates true north accurately enough for estimating direction. Another useful star is Benetnasch (No. 39). Neither of these stars is among those listed as the brightest, or of the first magnitude, but are included because of their usefulness to the air navigator. The twenty-two other navigator's stars are :

No.	Name	Abbreviation	No.	Name	Abbreviation
1.	Achernar	Achar	12.	Dubhe	—
2.	Acrux	—	13.	Fomalhaut	Fomalt
3.	Aldebaran	Aldeban	14.	Peacock	—
4.	Alpheratz	Alphaz	15.	Pollux	—
5.	Altair	—	16.	Procyon	—
6.	Antares	—	17.	Regulus	—
7.	Acturus	Arctus	18.	Rigel	—
8.	Betelgeuse	Betelus	19.	Rigel Kent	Rikent
9.	Canopus	—	20.	Sirius	—
10.	Capella	—	21.	Spica	—
11.	Deneb	—	22.	Vega	—

To an observer on the earth the heavenly bodies appear to circle our globe once nearly every twenty-four hours. In fact, they reach the same place in the sky four minutes earlier every day—which explains why the " pattern " is always changing. Star movements and position changes are regular and orderly, and have been the object of so much study over so many centuries that the position which any given heavenly body will have in relation to the earth at any given moment can be forecast with extreme accuracy for years and years to come.

Eclipses of the sun and moon can be predicted long before they occur, for the same reason.

The day-to-day positions of the heavenly bodies used by the R.A.F. air navigator are published in a document known as the Air Almanac.

This comes out three times a year, and by using an up-to-date edition the navigator is saved the trouble of working out the change that has taken place since the date of any earlier issue which he may have in his possession.

FINDING THE WAY IN THE AIR

To discover his position, the navigator must make two or more "observations," and while he is busy with his sextant the aeroplane must be flown as straight and level as possible and at a steady speed. Usually, the human pilot hands over to the automatic pilot when the navigator is "shooting" the stars.

Navigators use the stars for taking bearings in much the same way as they use objects on the surface. Because the positions of the stars at the time of observation are known, or can be found out, they provide information upon which position lines can be drawn. "Shots" at three well-spaced stars give an accurate "fix."

To simplify this work as much as possible, the navigator has an astrodome, a rounded glass-covered canopy on the roof of the fuselage in close proximity to his station in the aeroplane. By standing with his head and shoulders in the 'dome, he can command a wide view of the heavens and use his sextant under the best possible conditions. A new kind of sextant, now coming into use, makes possible the taking of astronomical observations without the use of an astrodome.

Radio and radar, which are dealt with in the next chapter, are extensively used in air navigation, but these aids do not excuse the navigator from learning the art of finding his way in the air without them. Periodically, the Royal Air Force embarks upon exercises that may send one or more crews on flights of several thousand miles, either to test the navigator's skill or to try out some new device, method or technique which might improve the general standard of navigational skill in the Service and make crews yet more independent of help from the ground.

From this brief excursion into a very complex and difficult subject, it is clear that navigation is an art calling for a high degree of intelligence and a quick brain. Obviously, the navigator's job is as important as the pilot's. This is acknowledged by the authorities, and is proved by the fact that a navigator often captains an aeroplane and can command a squadron. Therefore, if the Royal Air Force thinks that you would make a good navigator when you had set your heart on being a pilot, do not be disappointed. Your selection for training in navigation is a glowing compliment to your abilities, and your career as a navigator will be little different from that as a pilot.

EXPLAINING THE MYSTERIES OF RADAR TO YOUNG AIRMEN.

THE EARS, VOICE AND EYES OF THE AEROPLANE

TO-DAY, radio-less aeroplanes are few and getting fewer. There are so many occasions when the aeroplane needs to speak to the ground and the ground to the aeroplane, and aeroplanes to each other, that the absence of radio is almost a danger ! Soon, radar, too, may be almost as essential. The days of the aeroplane which is deaf, dumb and blind are numbered.

The sciences of both radio and aeronautics have grown up together. The basic principles of aircraft construction, and the theory of flight, were first explained by Sir George Cayley, who lived from 1773 to 1857 and was later hailed as " the Father of British Aeronautics." Soon after his death, another scientist, James Clerk-Maxwell, proved by mathematical calculation that electromagnetic

131

waves travelled through space at the speed of light. Thirty years later his theory was proved correct, and by 1889 signals carried on electromagnetic waves had been transmitted across the English Channel—a very notable achievement. The Wireless Age dawned at the turn of the century, and so did the Air Age.

To develop the military use of the new means of communication, the War Office formed a Wireless Company of the Royal Engineers. Experiments to test the feasibility of using wireless to and from flying machines were first made by this company with a tethered balloon. Later a free balloon was used and signals were exchanged over a distance of 30 miles. As time went on the experiments were extended to airships, and the difficulties created by a noisy engine at once became apparent. The airship could transmit its signals and the signals could be received clearly enough by the ground station, but if the airship wished to hear what the ground station had to say its engine had to be stopped.

Later, attempts were made to establish wireless communication between the ground and aeroplanes. Again it was found possible to transmit from the aeroplane, but signals from the ground could be heard only when the aeroplane shut off its engine.

Then came earphones, and the main obstacle to two-way wireless communication between powered flying machines and the ground was removed. In 1913, two aeroplanes set off from Netheravon, on Salisbury Plain, and, flying on parallel courses 10 miles apart, exchanged signals with each other all the way to Bournemouth, while a ground station " listened in."

The probable military value of wireless was dramatically revealed in some pre-war army manœuvres. Two wireless-equipped airships were to have taken part, one on each side, but one broke down and the side without air support was so completely outmanœuvred by the other that the " war " came to an end a day earlier than had been planned. The airship had kept close watch on the " enemy " and reported his every move by wireless. There had been no chance of a surprise attack or a smart counter-stroke.

Then came the 1914–18 War. Wireless-equipped aeroplanes in the R.F.C. and R.N.A.S. were few, and those available could not be used until the German advance had been checked. But the advantage of wireless communication from the air soon became clear, particularly for reporting the accuracy of artillery fire. Thus,

By courtesy of]   [A. V. Roe & Co. Ltd.

THE WELL-EQUIPPED STATION OF THE PUPIL RADIO OPERATOR IN THE
ANSON TRAINER.

most wireless-equipped aeroplanes of those days worked with the gunners, "sitting" above a target and sending a "flying commentary" by Morse Code telling the gunners where their shells were falling. Here is an extract from a pilot's log book recording a "shoot" which took place in September, 1914.

4.2 p.m.	A very little short. Fire, fire.
4.4 p.m.	Fire again ; fire again.
4.12 p.m.	A little short ; line O.K.
4.15 p.m.	Short. Over. Over and a little left.
4.20 p.m.	You were just between two batteries. Search two hundred yards each side of your last shot. Range O.K.
4.22 p.m.	You have them.
4.26 p.m.	Hit. Hit. Hit.
4.32 p.m.	About 50 yards short and to the right.
4.37 p.m.	Your last shot in the middle of three batteries in action ; search all round within 300 yards of your last shot and you have them.
4.42 p.m.	I am coming home now.

Spelling out each word was a lengthy process, and there was soon devised a system of signalling which merely called for a letter and a number from the observing aeroplane to indicate the exact fall of each shell in relation to the target. Later, still better systems were evolved, and all through the war the wireless-equipped aeroplane was highly popular with the artillery. It doubled and trebled the effectiveness of a bombardment and enabled gunners to follow a target if it moved. But the Germans soon made "Art. Obs." (short for Artillery Observation) one of the more hazardous occupations in a military pilot's life, and our airmen had to fight for the right to sit on targets and dictate directions to the gunners. Only the side which had local command of the air could do the sitting.

Under the impetus of war, the expanding radio industry made rapid technical progress, and by 1918 sets had been made which could transmit voices instead of the dots and dashes of the Morse Code. This was an achievement of the greatest military as well as scientific significance. To untrained ears the sounds that reached the headphones more closely resembled the squawks of a strangled duck than a human voice passing a message, but the ear soon grew accustomed to the strange noises and made sense out of them.

THE ANSON TRAINER'S RADIO OPERATOR'S STATION.

Showing trailing aerial reel on the left, the Morse key on the right of the table and facilities for either
wireless telegraphy or radio telephony.

THE EARS, VOICE AND EYES OF THE AEROPLANE

Priority in the distribution of the wonderful new instruments of communication was given to the Home Defence squadrons. The Germans were still raiding the British Isles with their bombing 'planes, and the new form of wireless—called Radio Telephony—was a powerful aid to the pilots whose job it was to intercept the raiders.

It was a faster means of communication than the Morse Code and would have been even faster but for the need to speak every message twice over to make sure that it had been heard and understood, and the need also to announce one's intention of either sending or receiving.

The use of Morse, however, was not discontinued, and it still forms the principal means of long-distance communication in the Royal Air Force.

Wireless was originally developed purely for the sending and receiving of messages. Then it became a valuable instrument of navigation. If two (or preferably three) ground stations can pick up a signal radiated from an aeroplane, the position of the aeroplane can be found by intersecting the position lines indicating the bearing of the aeroplane in relation to the receiving stations. This method of locating the position of an aeroplane is known as Direction Finding, and any pilot or navigator who gets lost can ask for his position by contacting the appropriate ground station and, at the latter's request, sending out a signal long enough for his bearings to be taken. Seconds only are then needed to find out and give the aeroplane its position.

Later, by another device, aeroplanes were able to find their own position. This device is a rotable " homing " or " loop " aerial which can be brought to bear upon a transmitting station whose position is known. Usually, nowadays, this is an automatic beacon which transmits continuously and sends out an identification signal. As the aerial is turned so the signals received by it fade and grow in volume, just as they do when you turn a portable radio set on its turntable. By noting the positions at which maximum and minimum strength signals are received, the navigator can discover the bearing of the transmitting station and draw a position line. By using the rotable *and* the fixed aerial (the one normally used by the aeroplane for transmitting and receiving signals) he can discover whether the aeroplane is flying towards or away from the transmitting station—in other words, to add " sense " to direction.

By courtesy of]   *[Dept. of Scientific & Industrial Research*

AT WORK IN THE RECEIVING ROOM OF A C.H. STATION.

The course to be flown can then be worked out. Alternatively, the pilot may wish to fly so that he will arrive over the beacon, and then make his way from there. In that case he can bring into use a visual indicator which will instantly tell him if he strays from the beam, and also let him know the moment the aeroplane passes over the beacon. Some aeroplanes do not have a loop aerial, and therefore call up for a fix by D/F or some other method. The ability of an aeroplane to locate its own position, naturally, eases the task of the ground stations, and leaves them free to assist those with no other means of finding out where they are.

THE " SEEING EYE " OF RADAR

After radio telephony came the miracle of radar, and the aeroplane was given eyes to see with. Radar, like wireless and radio broadcasting, started life on the ground with large, clumsy and complicated apparatus. The principle upon which it works had been discovered some fifty years earlier by a German scientist, but it was British scientists who first put it to practical use. The German found that a radiated signal in the form of a " pulse " throws back an " echo " when it strikes a solid or near-solid object, and that it is possible to " catch " the echo on suitable apparatus. The British scientists found ways not only of catching the echo, but of measuring the distance travelled by the signal before hitting an object and of finding the position of the object which caused the echo.

When radar became a practical and reasonably efficient system of detection, Europe was living under the growing threat of war. Experiments had proved that aeroplanes could be " picked up " by radar over a distance of some 160 miles. It was therefore only logical that, while experiments still continued for radar's improvement, a chain of radar stations should be set up round England's coasts as a measure of defence. Thousands of people must have seen these strange structures going up, and even watched them being tested, without suspecting their nature or purpose. Radar was one of the country's best-kept secrets, and not until we had been at war for more than a year was the existence of this wonderful, silent, and almost infallible weapon disclosed.

The name by which it was first made known to the public was " radiolocation," but the Americans changed it to radar, and radar it has remained ever since.

Every scientist who could be spared was set to work on radar, and in a short time new discoveries paved the way for equipment small enough to be fitted into an aeroplane—a technical triumph which hardly seemed possible when radar was first invented. Ranking high among them, if not holding the most important place of them all, is the cavity magnetron, a valve of small dimensions capable of giving a very high output—a thousand times more than the valves previously used.

Radar, and adaptations of radar, took many forms and fulfilled many roles. Among other things, the principle was used in equipment designed to identify a friendly aeroplane from one that was hostile, to assist bombers to find their targets, to warn bombers of the presence of enemy fighters, to keep bombers on course, and to bring them back to base ; in apparatus for detecting the presence of enemy bombers, and equipment for use by anti-aircraft guns. Radar, in fact, became universal and was widely used by both the Army and the Navy as well as by the Royal Air Force.

One form of war-time radar now has an important commercial responsibility. That is Ground Controlled Approach, a landing aid which brings aeroplanes to within a foot or two of the runway when the weather " shuts down " and hides the airfield from the pilot's view. The aeroplane carries no radar; it is brought in by

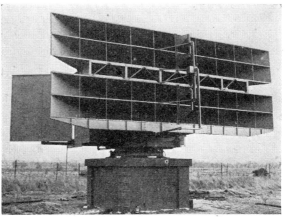

[*By courtesy of Dept. of Scientific and Industrial Research.*

HORIZONTAL " CHEESE " AERIAL.

instructions radioed to the pilot by the ground controller, who, watching his radar screen, knows exactly the aeroplane's position relative to the runway, and is thus able to guide the pilot although no more able to see the aeroplane than the pilot is able to see the runway through the murk and haze.

That, then, is a brief outline of the history of wireless telegraphy, radio telephony and radar as it concerns the Royal Air Force. It goes without saying that the R.A.F. still makes wide use of these aids to navigation, location and communication, and that their importance also makes important those who operate and keep serviceable the many different kinds of apparatus that come under this heading. Both operators and mechanics have to understand the working of the sets and to be well versed in their construction. This calls for a long and thorough training, but the course of instruction has the additional merit of being absorbingly interesting even to those for whom, at the start, electricity is one of life's bigger mysteries.

[*By courtesy of Dept. of Scientific and Industrial Research.*

COMBINATION RADAR AERIAL.

THE EARS, VOICE AND EYES OF THE AEROPLANE

Electromagnetic waves travel at the rate of 186,000 miles a second. For all practical purposes they can be assumed to travel at a constant speed; that is, their fastest and slowest speeds are almost the same. If they were visible, and much slowed down, they would resemble the waves or ripples set up by a pebble thrown into the smooth waters of a lake or pond. As the ripples vary in size according to the size of the stone dropped into the water, so electromagnetic waves vary in size according to the oscillations set up by oscillating circuits within the set.

They can also be said to resemble sound waves. Sound waves vary in size, too, and are usually measured by the frequency of their vibrations. The high-pitched note which we get from the top of the piano keyboard has a high frequency, the deep note from the bottom of the keyboard—which rumbles like distant thunder—has a low frequency.

We have grown into the habit of classifying electromagnetic waves in terms of wavelengths *and* frequencies. For convenience, we have divided these wavelengths and frequencies into the following groups, and in order to keep the figures within manageable limits, we use the symbol " kc/s " (kilocycles) to indicate so many thousand " cycles " (or vibrations) a second, and " mc/s " (megacycles) to indicate so many million " cycles " a second.

Very Low Frequencies (*VLF*): Below 30 kc/s. Greater than 10,000 metres.

Low Frequencies (*L/F*): 30–300 kc/s: 10,000–1,000 metres.

Medium Frequencies (*M/F*): 300–3,000 kc/s: 1,000–100 metres.

High Frequencies (*H/F*): 3–30 mc/s: 100–10 metres.

Very High Frequencies (*VHF*): 30–300 mc/s: 10–1 metres.

Decimetre Waves (*dc/W*): 300–3,000 mc/s: 1 metre–10 centimetres.

Centimetre Waves (*cm/W*): 3,000–30,000 mc/s: 10–1 centimetres.

This table shows that as frequency increases wavelength decreases.

The human ear can receive every sound which has a frequency (or wavelength) within its compass, and does not have to be adjusted for each sound. A radio receiver hears only the wavelengths or frequencies to which it is attuned, and for this reason it is fitted with means for changing the sensitivity of its ears to the precise wavelength on which its operator wishes to listen. Similarly, a predetermined wavelength is used for transmitting.

There are so many users of radio transmitters in the world that wavelengths have had to be allotted in such a way—by international agreement—that there is little or no overlapping between any two stations within transmitting distance of one another. If this were not done, all would be chaos, and radio as a means of communication would be useless. The R.A.F., in common with other users, has its allotted wavebands and allocates them to its ground stations and aircraft in the manner best suited to their varying functions. The distance travelled by electromagnetic waves depends upon their frequency and the power used in transmitting them. Some have no more than " optical " range, which means that they are effective only to the distance that can be seen from the transmitting aerial.

In wireless telegraphy and radio telephony the ear is the most important sense ; in radar it is the eye that takes in the message.

Radar's "picture" is built

[By courtesy of Dept. of Scientific and Industrial Research.
RADAR EQUIPMENT " CHAIN HOME " LOW STATION.
Used for offensive and defensive purposes.

up on the fluorescent inner surface of a cathode ray tube as it is bombarded by a stream of electrons—particles of negative electricity—travelling at tremendous speed. The bombardment causes the fluorescent surface to light up and to reproduce signs and signals in such a way that the trained observer can interpret them at a glance. In some ways, the radar screen resembles a television screen.

The radar aerial sends out its pulses at a rate suited to the kind of work the set is designed to do. Some send their pulses at the low rate of 25 a second, some as rapidly as 1,200 a second, but most kinds of radar used by the Royal Air Force send at speeds between 200 to 600 pulses a second. The more rapid the rate the more detailed the information sent back, but in no instance must the rate be so fast that a pulse leaves the aerial before the echo of the one in front has had time to return. If it leaves too soon the picture will be confused and useless.

Why this is so can be proved by a simple experiment. If you give a short loud shout when facing a cliff or wall, or when beneath the span of a large bridge, you hear the echo sharp and clear, but if you keep on shouting you hear no echo because of the noise you are making. Radar needs that tiny fraction of time in spacing for the echo to come back—if it is coming.

Naturally, the measurement of time in radar has to be very exact; it takes a pulse only 10·75 millionths of a second (or a little more than the one-hundred-thousandth part of a second) to reach an object one mile distant and for its echo to return. The one-millionth part of a second (or "microsecond," as it is called) is a common unit of time measurement in radar, and makes possible the astonishingly accurate results which can be obtained in finding the distance between the transmitting station and a reflecting object.

Some forms of radar use a "time base," which appears as a straight line of light on the screen. On it the position or distance (or both) of the reflecting object is shown as a "blip" or kink. Some forms of radar reproduce the features of land and coast lines in such a way that the detail on the screen can be used, in conjunction with a map, for navigational purposes.

There are two types of screen. On one the "display" disappears the instant that the electrons cease bombarding the fluorescent surface of the cathode ray tube. The other holds the impression long enough for the observer to note all the detail in which he is interested.

The "persistent" screen is used principally with systems which employ revolving aerials. Reflecting objects send back their echoes as they come within the beam of pulses. As soon as the beam has passed, the representation of the reflecting objects on the screen disappears and does not reappear until the beam strikes them again. Something similar would happen if the beam from a light-

[*Official Air Ministry Photo.*

RADAR MECHANICS SERVICING A MAIN AERIAL AT A GCI STATION.

house could photograph everything it lights up and present the scene to the lighthouse keeper on a cinema screen.

Not until the wonders of radar were officially revealed could the public understand some of the miraculous events of the war years. For instance, when the Luftwaffe began to suffer increasing losses in their night raids on the British Isles the story was put around that our night-fighter pilots were eating an abundance of carrots in order to improve their night vision. That was a reasonable enough explanation because carrots—raw carrots, in particular —actually contain substances that help people to see better in the dark. But non-carrot-eating pilots probably disposed of as many German raiders as did the carrot-eaters; good " night vision " in this case was not related to diet. One outstandingly successful night-fighter pilot was called " Cat's Eyes," and for years after the war he was known—chiefly to newspaper reporters—by that nickname.

Some of the principles of radar are embodied in other navigational aids for both aeroplanes and ships. These aids transmit pulses from ground stations but do not use the echo principle. Their position is known to the receiver of the signals, and by referring to the special maps or charts associated with the system, the navigator is able to find his position and to use their guidance in reaching a selected point.

Some of these systems are accurate to within a few hundred yards over distances of two or three hundred miles. They normally work in " teams " of three or four.

Of all the radar devices and devices using radar principles, none is more interesting to the airman than the type of equipment known as H_2S in one form and as A.S.V. in another. " H_2S " is, as you probably know, the chemical symbol for hydrogen sulphide, which has a smell like rotten eggs. This odd title for the radar system was not the first choice. Originally, it had been known by the code letters " B.N.," for " Blind Navigation." But the story goes that a well-known scientist asserted, when this form of radar was under discussion, that it ought to have been in use long before, and added that " the whole thing was stinking through not having been done years ago." Whereupon his colleagues promptly re-named the system H_2S—proving that scientists are not without a sense of humour, even though, in this instance, it tied a libellous label upon a remarkable piece of airborne equipment which, to some noses, appears quite odourless. In point of fact, H_2S could not have been developed earlier because the extremely short wavelength it needs was not available.

The influence of H_2S on the progress of the air war was little short of miraculous, and the system has been described as " the most brilliant of the infants of radar." After the first raid by bombers equipped with it, Headquarters, Bomber Command, concluded that " . . . H_2S is the most successful blind navigation and bombing aid yet devised." This weighty commendation was delivered some time after other remarkable bombing and blind navigation devices had been tested and proved efficient to a degree far greater than had been expected—devices which, in some instances, remained in use until the end of the war and some of which are still active now.

" A.S.V."—Air/Surface Vessels—was used with devastating effect against the German U-boats. In March, 1943, after Allied shipping losses by submarine had sometimes reached 800,000 tons a month, the first Coastal Command bombers to carry the new radar took off from Chivenor Airfield. Within a few nights several U-boats had been found and attacked on the surface, and from then onwards, as Mr. J. G. Crowther and Mr. R. Whiddington have told us in their fascinating book, *Science at War*, " the U-boats were slaughtered."

Allied shipping losses fell from 700,000 tons in March to less than 100,000 tons in August. The Chief of the German Navy frankly admitted that we had deprived his submarines of their essential feature—the element of surprise—by means of radar.

The principal merit which distinguishes H₂S from all other forms of airborne radar is its complete independence. It is, in fact, a self-contained, self-sufficient radar station, and one, fortunately, which the enemy can do little to interfere with. Other systems can sometimes be made unreliable or misleading by counter

By courtesy of]   [*Dept. of Scientific and Industrial Research.*
HEIGHT-FINDING EQUIPMENT.

measures, but H₂S is almost immune, because its wavelength is so short.

Its drawbacks are its size and complexity, its weight and the delicate nature of many of its costlier parts. There are twelve different units, each with a vital function to perform. Between them they weigh the best part of half a ton. Further, their operators need long and thorough training before they can become " operational." Nevertheless, there is no other piece of equipment which does what H_2S can do, and therefore the complication, the weight, the long training period, must all be regarded as the price which the system demands in payment for the services it renders.

In the war years H_2S advanced rapidly, and even now improvements are still being made to it. Doubtless, as time goes on, complication, weight and the operator's training period will grow less, and the value of the equipment raised still higher.

H_2S has a screen (known as the Plan Position Indicator because it indicates the exact location of the various objects and features whose reflections appear on it) which presents its observer with a " display " resembling a map of the territory being probed, or scanned, by pulses transmitted from a revolving aerial. The echoes thrown back by the various features of the land or water which the pulses strike build up a picture which an observer, by comparing it with a map of the area covered, can interpret, and thus keep track of his position.

The display is presented on a " persistent " type of screen. The picture is " drawn " by a revolving arm which, moving in tune with the aerial, makes a circuit of the screen about once every second—although the rate can be varied. This arm can be likened to the minute hand of a clock, except that it " sweeps " the dial very much faster. When echoes are coming in strongly, the arm seems to throw off pieces of brightly burning material which glow for a moment then die away.

Thus, the observer sees only a small section of the map at any given moment, but his training teaches him to visualize the whole scene. In any case, every detail of the picture is re-built about sixty times a minute, so that an observer does not have long to wait until he can check and re-check any detail about which he has doubts.

The picture is presented in black and white, like an ordinary photographic print or the presentation one sees on a television screen. Calm water throws back the weakest echoes. Land masses are more responsive ; built-up areas reflect powerfully. Thus, calm water does not light up the screen and is represented by dark areas. Land throws back fairly weak signals and appears as a grey shadow. Buildings, particularly those with metal in their construction, reflect strongly and appear on the screen as very bright patches. Sometimes indications are misleading. Two metal

By courtesy of]   [*" Flight."*
The " Radome " which houses the H_2S scanner of the Lincoln bomber is placed slightly aft of the bombing bay, here
seen with its doors open.

hangars can throw back echoes with the intensity of a small town, and the operator must guard against being deceived by mere brightness.

If an observer wishes to identify some particular feature, he has means for increasing or decreasing the intensity and sharpness of the display. For instance, when making a landfall after flying over the sea he may wish to sharpen the outline of the coast in order to recognize every detail and, by means of a map, make sure of his exact position. Later, he may wish to pick out certain towns or other landmarks. Controls for meeting his varying needs are included in the H_2S equipment.

Another control enables him to vary the area covered by the display so that he can adjust it to the scale of the map which he wants to use for some particular purpose. Thus, he is not bothered by the need to allow for differences in size of presentation; that which is represented on the screen is also represented on the map and to the same scale.

THE EARS, VOICE AND EYES OF THE AEROPLANE

H_2S includes another valuable aid—an indication of the course being flown. This is set when the aeroplane starts its journey and the apparatus which controls it is linked with the compass. Every time the " minute hand " falls along the course, a thin line, radiating from the centre to the edge of the screen, is brightly illuminated for a moment. The observer is thus able to give the pilot exact instructions as to course—a facility which is very useful when precise navigation is called for.

During the war, bombers were guided by other navigational aids using radar principles, but it was to H_2S that Bomber Command and Coastal Command of the Royal Air Force owed their greatest triumphs.

With its penetrating eye, able to pierce cloud, fog and mist, this remarkable piece of airborne equipment enabled bombers to find their targets whatever the weather. On 3rd December, 1943, Leipzig was bombed through dense fog, and the accuracy of the bombing was proved later by photographs taken by reconnais-

By courtesy of]   [Vickers-Armstrongs, Ltd.

THIS ROOMY COCKPIT BELONGS TO A VICKERS VALETTA TWIN-ENGINED TRANSPORT

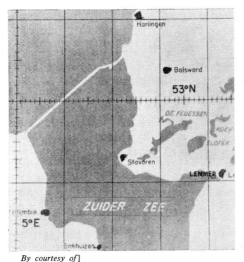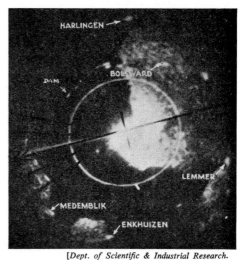

By courtesy of]　　　　　　　　　　　[Dept. of Scientific & Industrial Research.

A MAP OF THE ZUIDER ZEE AND (*right*) THE SAME AREA PHOTOGRAPHED FROM AN H₂S " DISPLAY."

sance aircraft. Not one of the bombers taking part in that raid could have caught even a glimpse of the ground, yet all the bombs had fallen into the target area.

Berlin had always been fairly easy to find, but when every bomb had to do the maximum amount of damage it was necessary that small districts should be recognized. By the end of 1943, sufficient detail could be assembled on the Plan Position Indicator of H_2S to make identification of localities certain. During the six months which ended in March, 1944, some 93 per cent. of the R.A.F.'s strategic bombing effort depended on navigation and bombing with the aid of H_2S. If the methods and facilities of the earlier years had had to be relied upon, the war might have dragged on for years longer, simply because so much of the effort involved would have been wasted.

Further, when radar devices became available, the R.A.F. suffered fewer losses ; in fact, the casualty rate became so low that, after 1943, thousands of workers in aircraft factories were switched to other activities. The R.A.F. had all the aircraft it could operate, and plenty in reserve.

When the official history of the war in the air in World War II is written, a big place will be given to the part of radar. It was, indeed, one of the most powerful instruments of allied victory.

A group of candidates at a Selection Centre undergoing a test designed to disclose whether their hearing and powers of comprehension are up to R.A.F. standards.

MEN FOR AIRCREW DUTIES

THOSE candidates who pass the aircrew examinations and tests set by the R.A.F. can be certain that they are in pretty good shape physically, mentally and temperamentally. The odd thing is that so many young men of contrasting type manage to get through them. Because the standards are so high and so closely defined, one would imagine that those who were successful would be so much alike that they might have been cast in the same mould, like minted coins. But pick out a dozen of them at random and you will find twelve men with different physical dimensions, different temperaments, different educational attainments and different outlooks. There is no " sameness " about them.

A high physical standard has always been insisted upon since military flying began. Flying an aeroplane does not call for great strength, and there is no need for would-be pilots to build up a muscular system resembling that of a blacksmith or a champion weight-lifter. But eyes must be keen as a hawk's, the heart sound and lungs well-nigh perfect. All the numerous other organs of the body must be functioning properly and must show no trace of ever having been seriously out of order. Evidence of certain illnesses and diseases can disqualify a candidate, and so can failure to meet certain height and leg-length stipulations. In fact, a glance through the list of conditions laid down can be startling, and it is a tribute to the modern generation that so many young men pass the examination with flying colours.

The doctors are very thorough. Candidates are passed from one specialist to another as ears, eyes, nose, throat, lungs and all the rest are tested. This examination takes a full half-day. Statistics collected over a long period prove that most of those who fail the examination usually come to grief on the eyesight test. This, naturally, has to be very stiff. For one thing, a pilot must be an expert judge of distance. Flying at 600 miles an hour he covers nearly 900 ft. (or 300 yd.) in one second. He cannot suddenly

[*Sport and General.*

CANDIDATES FOR AIRCREW DUTIES UNDERGOING APTITUDE TESTS AT A SELECTION CENTRE.

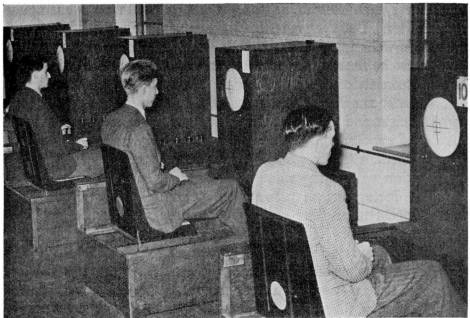

[*Sport and General.*

ANOTHER KIND OF APTITUDE TEST WHICH CANDIDATES FOR AIRCREW DUTIES HAVE TO TAKE.

slow down to judge distance in opening an attack on an enemy, or to take evasive action in an attempt to escape interception. He must size up the situation instantly, and swing his aeroplane into the one attitude or position that will bring him success.

Great stress is also placed on colour registration, and ingenious tests reveal whether candidates suffer from any form of colour blindness. The cockpit, maps, charts, navigation lights, pyrotechnic signals, all make demands upon the colour sense, and the slightest defect may lead to trouble. Thousands of people suffer some degree of colour blindness without knowing it, and the inability to identify colours correctly has caused many a candidate to fail the examination.

A sound bodily constitution and a good colour sense are not of themselves a passport to the flight deck. The candidate must also have an alert and responsive mind. Flying calls for very quick decisions. The man who needs time to make up his mind is useless. The successful pilot, navigator, signaller or flight engineer must be able to deal with a situation as it arises. In fact, some circumstances may have to be anticipated if they are to be successfully met—just as a good goal-keeper anticipates the intention of the centre-forward. The R.A.F. has many novel ways for discovering the candidate's speed of reaction. They are kept a close secret, and are constantly being varied so that candidates shall not get to know about them and work in a little advance practice !

Another human quality looked for is initiative. A pilot who is helpless when faced with an unexpected situation, or when left to his own resources, is no asset to a squadron, although he may be brilliant at aerobatics, or a wizard at cross-country flying. It was often noticed in World War II that both German and Japanese pilots were easy prey if they lost their leaders. With the leader gone, a formation would scatter and make for home, instead of keeping together at all cost, and defending each other. This may have sprung from a national characteristic or have been the result of imperfect training. Yet the leaders were nearly always skilful and often brilliant tacticians. The rest were like sheep.

War-time flying by day, whether in fighters or bombers, is largely a matter of team-work, and the team which can remain together longest is often the most successful. Nevertheless, the

[*Sport and General.*

These candidates for aircrew duties are not playing a single-handed game of draughts, but are undergoing one of the several aptitude tests designed to reveal the speed of their reactions and reasoning powers.

[*Sport and General.*

A CANDIDATE FOR AIRCREW DUTIES UNDERGOING A MEDICAL TEST AT AN R.A.F.
SELECTION CENTRE.

R.A.F. has always believed in making its pilots self-reliant so that they are not easy prey if they become separated or lose their leader and have to fight on their own or return to base without the protection of their companions.

" Born leaders " are few and far between. It does not follow that because a man is good at a certain task he should for that reason be appointed to a position of responsibility. The true leader is born, and he will always reveal himself when the test comes. The R.A.F. knows this, and has evolved a system which unfailingly brings to light the leaders among the candidates. The tests are of such a nature that the officious, the pompous, the boastful and the arrogant, who sometimes impress the more gullible, cannot be mistaken for leaders. Dross can never pass for gold. The leader reveals himself unconsciously and inevitably, and long experience has shown that those who are possessed of the qualities that make a man a natural leader almost invariably win promotion in their Service career rather more quickly than those who, though good at their job, are not cut out for responsibility and control or direction of others by example or command.

The process of aircrew selection takes several days, and at the end of it the selectors know more about the candidates than the candidates know about themselves. They have, as it were, put the candidates through a powerful and searching X-ray machine and scrutinized both bodies and minds. The R.A.F. system has been proved sound, and other air forces now use it. It is a lengthy and costly system, but it pays for itself over and over again. It eliminates any candidate who suffers from physical or mental shortcomings which might not be revealed by a less searching examination. It ensures that only the best are accepted for training. It reduces to a minimum the chance that a candidate will have to abandon his training before it is complete, thus saving the country much expense and the candidate a heartbreaking disappointment. Finally, it determines the kind of training for which each candidate is best suited, and prevents square pegs from getting into round holes.

Those who are chosen for pilot training probably count themselves luckiest. There is a lure and a fascination about the stick and rudder bar that will often make adventurous young men sacrifice more material things in exchange for the excitement, the thrill, the

[*Crown Copyright Reserved.*

A PUPIL PILOT, WEARING THE NOW-DISCARDED "LAUREL" BADGE LEARNING TO USE RADIO.

[Central Press.

PUPILS BEING SHOWN THE MECHANISM OF A MACHINE-GUN.

deep satisfaction that springs from the rise and swerve of a powerful aeroplane responding to the touch of a steady hand and a firm foot. We have already sampled, in imagination, the delights of a baptismal flight, and been instructed in the elementary principles of flying. The R.A.F. pupil pilot will settle down to a course of training which will last for seventy-six weeks, after which he will go through still more training before reaching an operational squadron.

The Royal Air Force's present system of flying instruction aims at following the syllabus very closely, regardless of weather. In some parts of the world the weather is easily predictable, and long calm, sunny periods enable a pupil's flying to be planned weeks ahead without much risk of interference from the weather. In Great Britain, weather is more erratic and at one time low cloud, fog and mist would often keep a pupil on the ground for days on end. To-day, the weather has to be extremely bad before it can bring flying lessons to a halt.

How very different from the early days of flying, when pupils and instructors had to be up at the crack of dawn to catch that fleeting moment of calm which often comes with the first light of a new day. If the smoke from the chimney was not almost vertical, or if the breeze fluttered a handkerchief, flying was " scrubbed " because the wind was much too boisterous.

Not all " flying " training is given in the air. There are, nowadays, ground devices which reproduce the conditions of flight so accurately that for certain purposes they can actually be used as a substitute for aeroplanes. One of the best known of these devices is the Link Trainer. Basically, this is an aeroplane's cockpit, but to make it appear more realistic it has a short blunt nose, a stumpy fuselage, a miniature tail and a couple of abbreviated wings—making a caricature of an aeroplane. The whole lot is mounted on a pedestal, and can be turned through 360 degrees and " banked " quite steeply, " dived " and " climbed."

Its original purpose was to teach pilots " blind " flying, or the art of navigating without external aids. Previously—because of the unreliability of human senses and the uncertain behaviour of some

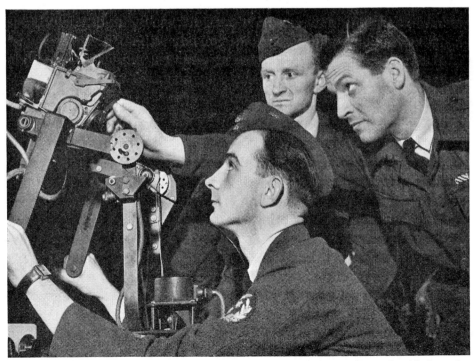

INSTRUCTION IN THE USE OF THE GYRO GUNSIGHT.

of the instruments—blind flying was not generally practised. Then came new instruments to supply, precisely, the information which the senses supplied unreliably, and experienced pilots had to be "converted" to blind flying so that they could tackle the kind of weather that robbed them of external aids to navigation, such as the horizon, the sun, the moon, and the ground. Teaching the pilot the new technique in the air was a costly business; the Link Trainer did the job just as well, at less cost and no risk.

Since it first appeared, the Link has fulfilled many other roles, but its chief function has always remained that of teaching the art of flying by instruments from take-off to landing. Its fidelity is amazing, and a pupil cannot fake a skill which he does not possess. Instruments respond to every movement of stick and rudder bar, showing increased height with climb, the rate of ascent, speed, bank and turn—everything is noted on the appropriate dial, even to spin and stall. The pupil might be happier if he could "fly" the Link alone—it is a single-seater—but that privilege is denied him. On the instructor's table is a set of instruments duplicating his own, and what his instruments record is shown, too, on those in front of the instructor. Thus, the Link is not really a single-seater!

One test of blind-flying skill is the triangular, or three-legged, cross-country flight in which the pupil "takes off" and, at a pre-arranged "speed" and with an assumed wind speed and direction, heads for a fixed point, turns round it, heads for the next, turns round that and heads for the departure point, to complete the triangle.

You want to know how the instructor can discover whether the pupil in the Link is flying the right course, making the right turns at the right moment and holding the right height to escape contact with high ground. That brings us to another feature of the Link Trainer—known colloquially as the Crab. This is an ungainly-looking object which has three travelling wheels, and can leave a trail of ink as it moves. It runs on a sheet of transparent material, under which is a map. It is started at a point on the map corresponding to the pupil's take-off point, and thereafter relentlessly follows whatever course the pupil steers. Thus, the instructor can leave the recording to the Crab, and does not have to check the pupil's flying mile by mile. The Crab often chastens an over-confident pupil by proving that, though he may be polished in his

AN INSTRUCTOR EXPLAINING THE OPERATION OF A GUN TO A
GROUP OF PUPILS.

aerobatics and landings, his navigation is atrocious. All blind flying is done " under the hood " so that the pupil is completely cut off from the world except by " radio " communication—which is sometimes real radio—from the instructor's table.

The Link can also give practice in the various radio landing aids which are in common use, including Ground Controlled Approach, the various navigational aids using radar principles, and beam approaches. The most widely used system is the beam approach, which by aural and/or visual signals guides the pilot in his landing approach.

In the aural system he hears one set of signals if he is to the right of the beam, another if he is to the left, and a third if he is " bang on." Superimposed signals tell him his distance from the airfield boundary. In the visual system two needles in a single dial tell him not only if he is " on the beam " but also if his rate of descent is correct. The attitude of the needles tell him the degree and direction of any error.

In the old days, pupils had to rely almost entirely upon lectures for their classroom instructions. Lectures were enlivened by the

[Crown Copyright Reserve.

THE FLIGHT ENGINEER AT HIS STATION IN A HASTINGS MILITARY TRANSPORT.

[*Crown Copyright Reserved.*

AIR GUNNERS IN TRAINING.
Learning to judge relative speed through reflector sights.

use of printed diagrams, and by diagrams and sketches chalked upon a blackboard. Pupils had to work their way through a small library of " manuals "—books designed to supplement and consolidate the knowledge imparted by the lecturers. To-day, classroom studies are more interesting and probably twice as effective because far wider use is made of scientific devices, such as wind and water tunnels and other means of demonstrating processes which are normally invisible to the naked eye and can otherwise be pictured only in the imagination.

Wind tunnels have long been in use both for instruction in aerodynamics and for aeronautical research. In their instructional use they are made to show how an airstream flows past a wing, a fuselage, a flat surface, a streamlined surface—anything, in fact, that has an aerodynamic significance.

Films, too, have a large part to play in the instruction of R.A.F. pupil pilots. The film may be based upon actual visible processes or, more often, upon the " animated strip," which is a popular method explaining the action or function of something which it is

A PUPIL GUNNER PRACTISING IN A TURRET.

impossible to photograph satisfactorily. The operation of a gas-turbine, which is difficult to explain in words, and impossible to photograph satisfactorily, can be made simple and clear by means of the animated diagram. Airflow, too, and " boundary layer " and similar phenomena can all be made plain by the cartoon or animated diagram.

In addition to aerodynamics, the pupil pilot learns the basic principles of aero-engines, airmanship, armament and meteorology, brushes up his mathematics, spends no less than 188 hours on navigation, 40 on physics, 116 on radio, and shorter periods on English, geography, the history of the R.A.F., the collection and use of information about the enemy (officially known as " intelligence "), and puts in a reasonable number of hours learning the art of discussion and debate as part of his training in citizenship. He attends physical training parades, takes part in mid-week and week-end sports and games, and usually finds time to indulge in his favourite hobby or pastime.

As he may one day have to help to defend his airfield against enemy attacks he learns the rudiments of soldiering—that is, how to handle a rifle and revolver, throw a hand grenade, take cover, advance and retreat in an orderly and professional manner, and how to engage in close combat and hand-to-hand fighting.

Thus we see why those who aspire to be R.A.F. pilots must be both physically fit and mentally alert and capable. The course of training is a testing one, and those not physically, temperamentally and educationally qualified would soon find themselves lagging behind the rest. The probability is that with all the time in the world at their command they would never complete the course.

TRAINING NAVIGATORS

A candidate's suitability for training as a navigator is discovered during his progress through the selection centre. If anything, the navigator must have educational attainments higher than those looked for in a pilot, so that, other things being equal, a candidate who had hoped to be chosen for pilot training might find himself picked for a navigator's course. This, as we mentioned earlier, is a direct compliment to him, and he need not fear that his superior

[Crown Copyright Reserved.

A " synthetic " gunnery trainer in which the pupil's targets are aircraft models moving across a realistically painted " backcloth."

mental powers will imperil his chances of promotion for the duration of his Service career. All the appointments open to a pilot are open to him, and there is a chance that he may, in due course, undergo pilot training too—rather as a Technical Branch officer undergoes training; that is, not for operational duties, but merely in order that he may understand and practise the art of flying.

Navigator pupils also make full use of " synthetic " training devices that give them " air experience " without their leaving the ground, but they also put in plenty of airborne training. Their first ventures into the air make them acquainted with map reading; later they fly by dead reckoning, then by radio, radar and other aids. Often, their pilots will make deliberate but subtle mistakes, and upon the pupil navigator falls the duty of discovering the aeroplane's position and prescribing the course to be flown to reach its intended destination. (The pilot is probably well aware of his position all the time, and will doubtless be back on the ground for tea whatever course the pupil navigator tells him to fly !)

Here are a few of the classroom subjects which the navigator studies during the first seventy-six weeks of his training : form of the earth; great circles; small circles; latitude; longitude; direction of the earth; true, magnetic and compass directions; variation; deviation; course; track; drift; bearing; triangle of velocities; importance of time in navigation; navigation instruments, including computors and sextants; maps and charts; compasses; flying instruments used by the navigator; astronomy; armament, including bomb sights, bomb carriers, bomb aimer's panel; bombs and their component parts; pyrotechnics; aircraft guns and gun turrets; meteorology; radio and radar; photography; aircraft recognition; physics and mathematics. He also takes the usual general subjects, learns to drill, and goes through a course of ground combat training.

TRAINING SIGNALLERS, FLIGHT ENGINEERS AND GUNNERS

The training of signallers takes only two weeks less than that of pilots and navigators. It is broken up into 2,200 periods, of which 1,180 periods are devoted to technical instruction, 150 periods to technical education, 871 to general service training, and 19 are needed for the formalities of arrival at and departure from the school.

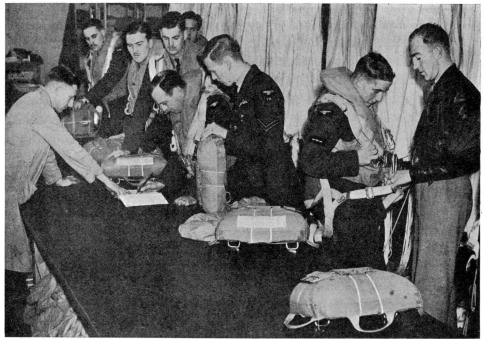

[*Fox Photos.*

AIRCREWS DRAWING THEIR PARACHUTES.

There are three stages, initial, basic and applied. The technical training given in the initial stage covers such subjects as: basic radio and electrical principles; R.A.F. airborne radio equipment; signalling; signalling procedure and aircraft electrical equipment. Technical education covers aerodynamics and aero-engines, English, geography, meteorology and mathematics. New subjects introduced during the basic stage under technical training include radio organization, synthetic operating training, communication flying, radar flying, flight ground training and daily servicing of instruments and equipment.

Signallers are also taught a good deal about guns and air firing, and about gun turrets and how they work. This is in case they have to take the place of a gunner who has become a casualty. Like other members of an aircrew he also has to be familiar with the working and wearing of parachutes and life-saving waistcoats, and with the self-inflating dinghies which are carried in all large Service aeroplanes—and how to get into them if forced to " ditch," that is, come down on the water. Signallers also have their own specialized forms of synthetic trainers, and complete a pretty good log of flying hours before going to an operational squadron.

Flight engineers also need seventy-four weeks for their training. They receive instruction on such matters as airframes, hydraulic and pneumatic systems, principles of aero-engine design and construction (piston and gas-turbine), ignition systems, carburettors and principles of supercharging, landing gears, electrical installations, instruments, propellers, the loading of aeroplanes, airmanship and flying safety, meteorology, aerodrome procedures, the theory of flight, the flying controls and, of course, the general educational subjects such as English, physics, geography and mathematics. Like the signaller, he, too, takes part in discussions and debates, and in sports and recreation.

Air gunners take a course made up of an initial stage of twenty weeks (858 periods), a basic stage of twenty-two weeks (936 periods) and an applied stage of twenty-one weeks (897 periods), the whole being broken up by leave periods amounting to six weeks. Many " aids " are used, including cine films, projectors, episcopes, sectioned models, diagrams, demonstrations and exhibitions. In the workshops the pupils are taught the construction and functioning of rifles, revolvers, machine-guns, gun turrets, gun and bomb sights, projectiles, pyrotechnics, bomb carriers, bomb-handling equipment, electrical equipment connected with armaments, radar and photographic equipment, the carriage of explosives in aeroplanes, and chemical weapons. Classroom studies include mathematics, mechanics, materials and heat, electrical theory, electronics, principles of flight and aero-engines. The characteristics of various ferrous and non-ferrous metals, methods of working them, the use of the principal hand and bench tools, the use of certain machine tools and the making and uses of screws, nuts and bolts—all these are in the syllabus.

The guns dealt with include the ·50-in. Browning gun and the 20-mm. Hispano. They learn to strip and assemble them, how to clear stoppages, make adjustments, and the working of the loading and firing mechanisms. They take English, geography, citizenship (a subject common to most R.A.F. courses) and the organization and administration of the R.A.F. They, like all the other pupils, play games, take part in sport and indulge in their favourite hobbies and pastimes.

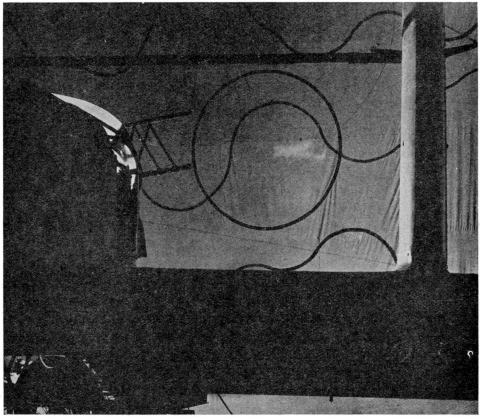

[*Planet News.*

NIGHT GUNNERY TRAINING.
A shadow plane moving on a screen is the gunner's target.

In 1946, the Royal Air Force introduced a new set of ranks for its non-commissioned pilots, navigators, signallers, engineers and gunners. When training they were known as cadets. The qualified pilot cadet became Pilot IV, and was subsequently promoted to Pilot III, Pilot II, and Pilot I. The highest non-commissioned rank he could reach was Master Pilot. Cadets in the other callings held similar ranks. Special badges, worn on the sleeve, indicated the rank held. These ranks and badges were never popular in the Service, and no one was surprised when, in 1950, the Air Ministry announced that the old ranks and badges were being revived and the new ones discarded—all except Master Pilot, Master Navigator and so on. So, stripes are back in fashion again, and aircrew are known by the titles they bore with pride and dignity for more than thirty years.

[*Fox Photos.*

A BOY APPRENTICE ADJUSTING THE TAPPETS OF A RADIAL AERO-ENGINE.

TENDING THE R.A.F.'s WARPLANES

NOT everyone who joins the Royal Air Force can become a pilot, navigator, signaller, flight engineer or gunner—or wishes to. There are scores of other jobs to be done, and apart from the fact that many young men could not pass the aircrew tests if they tried, some of the jobs on the ground are just as exciting as and equal in importance with those connected with flying. But the R.A.F.'s system of training often gives an airman the best of both worlds. It will often teach him to be a first-class mechanic and then, as the reward for good work, train him for the flight deck.

He is thus doubly qualified—as a highly skilled technician and a competent pilot or navigator. In this chapter we are to deal first and foremost with the engineers who see that the R.A.F.'s aeroplanes are kept in good working order.

From an earlier chapter we know that the large modern warplane is an extremely complex structure, built to very exact dimensions and filled with hundreds of instruments and accessories, yards of electric cable and hydraulic and pneumatic piping, all of the lightest possible materials yet robust enough to withstand vibration and the normal knocks and jolts of everyday service. To keep such an assembly of " bits and pieces " in good order demands the skilful hands of many mechanics, all of whom have to be trained to a high state of efficiency to perform a given set of duties, often in the least favourable conditions—particularly in war-time. In other words, the modern warplane calls for the services of many specialists, each

[Central Press.

PRACTICAL INSTRUCTION IN REPAIRS.

concerned with only one main item in the long list of parts that need constant and expert care in case it should one day fail and lead to the failure of a mission or the loss of an aeroplane and its crew.

Such care is necessary because few " flying repairs " can be made to an aeroplane while it is in the air. You cannot, as you can with a car, " get out and get under." Nothing can be more demoralizing to the ground crew, as well as to the aircrew, than their aeroplane being forced to turn back soon after setting out on a mission because some mechanical defect has developed and destroyed all chance of the aeroplane reaching its objective, let alone returning. That is why servicing and maintenance are so thoroughly stressed, and every practical step taken to ensure the complete operational efficiency of every part of the aeroplane. There are so many things that can " fail to function " and so many trivial causes of serious trouble.

A FITTER AT WORK ON THE ENGINE OF A JET FIGHTER.

Some people think that " servicing " and " maintenance " are one and the same thing, but that is not the case in the R.A.F. Servicing consists in completing those processes which have, in general, a day-to-day character ; for instance, under servicing come such routines as filling the oil and fuel tanks, replenishing the ammunition boxes, making small repairs, loading the bombs and rockets, recovering usable materials, instruments, equipment, etc., from crashed or damaged aeroplanes, and so on. Maintenance covers matters of production, supply, storage, overhaul, spares and

[Fox Photos.

INSTRUCTION ON AERO-ENGINES FOR AIRCRAFT APPRENTICES.

the wider aspects of salvage—the process of collecting items from wrecked or damaged aeroplanes and disposing of what remains.

In the Royal Air Force there are four " degrees " of servicing known, respectively, as First-line, Second-line, Third-line and Fourth-line. First-line servicing is done by semi-skilled " tradesmen " (the term used for all men who have qualified in a particular trade), assisted by unskilled men and supervised by skilled N.C.O. tradesmen. It consists of filling the fuel and oil tanks and other " replenishment " operations which are necessary; a brief but careful examination of the structure, engines and the various services to see that they are working properly, and such cleaning jobs as are needed; and the correction of defects which can be put right by the replacement of minor parts and by minor repairs. This routine is gone through before and after every flight.

Second-line servicing is done by skilled tradesmen assisted by semi-skilled men and to a lesser degree by unskilled men, all of whom are supervised by skilled N.C.O. tradesmen. It takes place when an aeroplane has completed a prescribed number of flying hours. The structure, engines and services are examined carefully for signs of deterioration or faults in operation. At the same time, repair jobs which are too big to be dealt with under first-line servicing are taken in hand—jobs which usually occupy from one to five days. Attention is also given to the various components to make sure that they are working properly.

Generally speaking, third-line servicing is the responsibility of skilled tradesmen, assisted by semi-skilled and unskilled men. These men undertake repairs which cannot be done by either first- or second-line servicing. They also retrieve as much usable material, instruments and equipment as possible from wrecked aeroplanes, and dispose of the remains of those which are so badly damaged that nothing usable can be taken from them.

Fourth-line servicing is done almost entirely by skilled trades-men. This consists of repairing aircraft and equipment damaged by accident; overhauling airframes and, if alterations are needed, making them. The men also overhaul engines and make them " as new " again for another spell of service. They examine and repair components, and in general do all the kinds of jobs that fall to the lot of the skilled aeronautical engineer in the R.A.F. Only the most skilful and most conscientious men are employed on fourth-line servicing.

It has often been said, with truth, that the ease or difficulty with which an aeroplane can be kept " serviceable " is as much a measure of its efficiency as are its flying qualities. The men and women who have to look after the R.A.F.'s planes are always grumbling at the aircraft and engine designers for not having done this or that in order to make their work easier. Designers, of course, do their best to simplify the servicing of their aeroplanes, but in the pursuit of per-formance or on the instructions of others they are apt to put an item in a certain place where it fits conveniently rather than in the place where it most suits the convenience of the ground crew who must look after it. If one studies the subject in detail one comes to the conclusion that designing for ease of maintenance is as important as designing for performance. An aeroplane that can fly at 600 or 700 miles an hour is not much good to an air force if it has to stay on the ground for long spells because mechanics must take half of it to pieces merely to get at one small but vital part that needs attention.

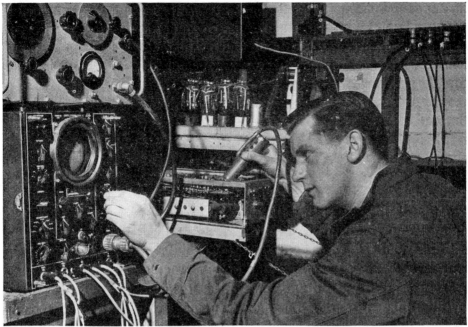

A RADIO MECHANIC TESTING EQUIPMENT.

The R.A.F. goes to great trouble to devise ways and means by which its aeroplanes can be serviced in the shortest possible time, and there is a special unit known as the Central Servicing Development Establishment (earlier known as the Air Ministry Servicing Development Unit) which does nothing but study servicing problems for every type of aeroplane which the Royal Air Force uses, and sets down on paper the routine which must be followed to get the work done efficiently and without waste of a single minute.

First, the C.S.D.E. collects all the information it can about a new type, and examines the data with great care before a specimen of the type arrives. If there is anything important which the advance information does not disclose the team of R.A.F. tradesmen who have taken a " manufacturer's course " on the aeroplane is called upon. These men have watched the aeroplane being built, and know it very thoroughly. When the new aeroplane arrives, the various expert mechanics—mostly skilled N.C.O.s (corporals, sergeants and flight sergeants)—go over it with great care, paying particular attention to those items on it which are their especial concern. A schedule of the items to be overhauled, and the periods of duty they will complete between overhauls, has been prepared in advance by the Government department which ordered the aeroplane, and this is the object of much consultation, because the purpose of the C.S.D.E. is to discover if, by how much, and how, the schedule can be improved upon so that more service can be obtained from the aeroplane in a given time. One hour saved on the servicing time of one aeroplane is something of a triumph, but only on the most reliable proof is a reduction of time or an extension of duty period sanctioned. Changes are not made for the sake of change.

When the " theoretical approach " has been completed—it may take ten days or more—the teams of experts put theory to test. They complete every job which will have to be completed when the aeroplane is in squadron service. They find out what tools will be needed, the best way of tackling a job, how long it takes, whether special tools might simplify a job, and so on. After one expert has completed a job, it is done again by another, and by yet a third, to make sure that it can be done in the same time and in the same way by more than one man. The entire aeroplane is " serviced " in this way from nose to tail, and then tests are made to discover how many men can work on the aeroplane at the same time without getting in each other's way. If you could watch the proceedings from beginning to end you might think that a lot of highly skilled men were wasting a lot of valuable time, and that it would be far better to let the men in the squadrons set about their jobs in their own way, cutting down their times as they got the knack of them. That was how it used to be done in the old days, and it seemed to work well enough then.

But you would be wrong. It is the bewildering complexity of the modern warplane that makes all this preliminary research work so vital. The pace of war has been steadily increasing during the past few centuries, and nowhere does war move faster than in the air. Every hour which an aeroplane spends unnecessarily on the ground undergoing repair is waste of effort as well as waste of time. The C.S.D.E. saves precious time, and if you want a striking example here it is. When the Short Sunderland flying-boat used to undergo a major inspection it was out of commission for fourteen working days. After it had been put through the C.S.D.E., it was found that the job could be done—and done properly—in only five days. The immediate result of the saving was that the R.A.F. had its fighting powers increased without the addition of a single aeroplane. Nine lost days had been retrieved because expert R.A.F. tradesmen had used their skill and experience to discover better ways for doing the job than those practised in the squadrons.

Just now we mentioned the conflict between aeroplane designers, who strive for the best possible performance in the air, and the men and women who have to keep the R.A.F.'s aeroplanes in fighting trim. Some designers pay heed to the "serviceability" of the aeroplanes, but others seem to assume that if something is put in the wrong place someone will soon start complaining and the thing will be put right. That happens often. For instance, there was a fighter on which it was impossible to remove the pneumatic bottle for draining without first removing the fuselage fuel tank and the hydraulic accumulator— a long, fiddling job. That could have been avoided by fitting the pneumatic

[Crown Copyright Reserved.
CORPORAL RADAR FITTER AT WORK.

bottle in another position or by incorporating a drain plug. No doubt when this was suggested, one or other of these alternatives was adopted. But a lot of trouble would have been saved if it had been done first. Examples of other difficulties of a similar nature are legion. On another fighter it was necessary to remove the blind flying panel before the flap control valve could be removed. On a third fighter it was necessary to remove the hydraulic header tank before the vacuum oil separators could be changed. To see to the airscrew's constant speed unit on a light bomber it was necessary to remove the whole engine cowling (which was in one piece), and to remove the cowling the airscrew had to be taken off. Thus many hours of work were necessary to complete a job that could have been done in a matter of minutes if the c.s.u. had been accessible. " Accessibility " is the basis of good servicing design.

These are the kind of " snags " which the highly skilled tradesmen of the C.S.D.E. have to find and try to overcome so that early steps can be taken to make the changes which will ease the burdens of those who have the responsibility of keeping the R.A.F.'s aeroplanes in tip-top working order. In the whole field of R.A.F. engineering there is probably no more interesting work to be found, and its worth to the R.A.F. and to the country can hardly be overestimated.

Although the C.S.D.E. does its best to guide every man and woman who has a servicing or maintenance job to do on an aeroplane it does not turn him or her into a robot, incapable of acting without instruction. The whole scheme of R.A.F. training encourages mechanics, just as it encourages pilots, to take the initiative at once if the textbooks and regulations do not provide ready or exact guidance. That is one of the secrets of the R.A.F.'s oft-demonstrated ability to keep going in conditions which might have proved too great a test for an air force trained to follow the " book of words " blindly.

The more important technical trades most closely concerned with the airworthiness of the R.A.F.'s aeroplanes are : Air Radio Fitter ; Blacksmith and Welder ; Carpenter ; Coppersmith and Sheet Metal Worker ; Electrician (Grade I) ; Fitter (Grade I) ; Fitter, Grade II (Engine) ; Fitter, Grade II (Airframe) ; Fitter (Armourer) ; Instrument Maker ; Radar Fitter (Air and Ground) ; and Wireless Fitter.

Men who serve in these trades form the technical " backbone " of the Royal Air Force. Many come into the Service from civil life wholly or partly trained, but the majority join as Aircraft Apprentices straight from school. Aircraft Apprentices normally complete twelve years service from the age of 18 years, and are usually allowed to " sign on " for another period and thus become eligible for a pension. Hundreds have qualified for commissions

TENDING THE R.A.F.'s WARPLANES

[*Crown Copyright Reserved.*

ELABORATE EQUIPMENT IS USED TO TEST THE ACCURACY OF AIRCRAFT INSTRUMENTS.

and have reached high rank and filled responsible positions, chiefly in some technical grade, and hundreds of others have become pilots and navigators, flight engineers, signallers and gunners.

An Aircraft Apprentice's training fills the best part of three years. It is extremely thorough and demands a high degree of diligence in the pupil. But do not imagine that the life of an apprentice is a life of ceaseless toil, of endless journeys from classroom to workshop and workshop back to classroom. Sports and games and recreations also have their part to play and every inducement and every encouragement are offered to get the apprentice, however studious he may be, out into the open to exercise his muscles and keep himself fit. In addition, there are clubs and societies for all the popular hobbies and pastimes normally followed by lads between the ages of $15\frac{1}{2}$ and 18.

Nor is all the training purely technical. The apprentice's general education is continued and extended, and he has facilities as good as, and often better than, those of his friends in civil life for broadening his knowledge. He attends lectures and takes part in debates and

By courtesy of]   *[" Flight."*

TWO EXAMPLES OF THE COMPLEX " PLUMBING " OF A MODERN AEROPLANE.

discussions on all manner of subjects, including politics. Thus, although he may have every intention of making the Royal Air Force his career, he is at the same time a man of the world with highly developed cultural tastes, able to talk confidently and well about things other than aeroplanes, verniers and spanners.

However, it is the technical instruction (practical and theoretical) that matters most, and the following notes give a fair indication of the subjects which the apprentices are taught for their respective trades.

The Instrument Maker : Mass, density, specific gravity, solids, rigidity, elastic properties, tensile tests, liquids, loss of fluid pressure, Bernouilli's theorem, the Bourdon tube, U-tube manometer, Hare's apparatus, Archimedes' principle, gases, pressure, simple barometer, Fortin barometer, barometer errors, aneroid barometer, applications of aneroid barometer in instruments, altimeter, variation of pressure with height.

Heat, potential difference and Ohm's law, cells, electromagnetism, electricity and heat, theory of flight, light, alternating current electricity, electronics, materials, mechanical properties of materials, tensile strength, ductibility, malleability, toughness, impact and fatigue resistance, heat treatment, mathematics, mechanics (forces, moments, mechanisms, velocity and acceleration, momentum, centrifugal and centripetal forces), gyroscopes, horology, energy, motion under gravity, power.

Electrical Fitters : General physics, electrical science, heat, internal combustion engines, materials, magnetism, direct current motors, electronics, applied mechanics, practical mathematics, engineering drawing, aerodynamics.

Fitter Armourer : Science (structure of matter, hydrostatics, heat, etc.), gun sights, magnetism, static electricity, current electricity, electromagnetism, direct current motors, explosives, the atmosphere, bomb sighting, light, aircraft gun sights, the piston engine, the gas-turbine, metallurgy, applied mechanics, practical mathematics, engineering drawing.

Engine Fitters : Science, fuels and combustion, carburation, supercharging, cooling, engines, hydrostatics, electricity, propellers, engine performance and efficiency, thermal efficiency, heat treatment,

["*Flight*" *Photo.*
THE NAPIER NOMAD 12-CYLINDER COMPOUND 2-STROKE HEAVY OIL AERO-ENGINE.
It is supercharged by a turbine-driven compressor.

strength of materials, jet propulsion, thermodynamics, force, work and power, velocity and acceleration, mechanics of flight, energy, machines, energy and momentum, gearing, angular motion, practical mathematics and engineering drawing.

Airframe Fitters : Science, hydrostatics, principles of flight, heat, electricity, materials of airframe construction, internal combustion engines, applied mechanics, practical mathematics, engineering drawing.

Air Radio Fitters : Mathematics, mechanics, mechanical drawing, basic radio principles, constitution of matter, solids, liquids, gases, molecules and atoms, atomic structure, the electron, proton and neutron, nuclear structure, isotopes, ions, free electrons, conductors and insulators, conduction current, potential difference, effects of a current, Ohm's law, Wheatstone's bridge, work, energy and power, thermo-electricity, thermo-junctions, ionization, electrolysis, cells, accumulator charging, magnetism, electromagnetism, magnetic properties of iron and steel, the magnetic circuit, the electric bell, the relay, field systems, static electricity and radar.

For their practical training the apprentices go to the workshops, where they are taught how to handle the tools of their trade and get practice in the jobs they will later do in the squadrons. At first, their " patients " are old airframes and engines whose service days are over, but towards the end of their training, when they have acquired a measure of manual dexterity, they receive instruction on types in squadron use. The same principle applies to all grades of Aircraft Apprentices—old and out-of-date equipment at first, the latest to bring them into touch with modern practice and procedures when they are about to qualify.

Other training schemes provide the Royal Air Force with its supply of " mechanics." For instance, there are Air Radar Mechanics, Air Wireless Mechanics, Flight Mechanics (Airframe), Flight Mechanics (Engines), Ground Radar Mechanics, Ground Wireless Mechanics and so on. One scheme caters especially for boys who have just left school. This trains them to be Airframe Mechanics, Armament Mechanics, Electrical Mechanics, Engine Mechanics or Instrument Mechanics.

When they join, these lads are called " Boy Entrants," and they may sign on for eight years' regular service and four years on the reserve, nine years' regular and three reserve, ten years' regular and

TENDING THE R.A.F.'s WARPLANES

[Crown Copyright Reserved.

A FLIGHT SERGEANT INSTRUCTOR EXPLAINING THE OIL SYSTEM OF THE MERLIN ENGINE.

two reserve, or for a full spell of twelve years' regular service and no reserve. This, however, is not the longest term the Boy Entrant can serve. In favourable conditions he might stay in uniform until, like men in other trades, he is 55 years old and qualified for a worthwhile pension.

With most others who join the Royal Air Force, he has the chance of winning a commission, of being chosen for aircrew duty, or both. So those who, for any reason, cannot or do not wish to join as Aircraft Apprentices may find a way into the R.A.F. as Boy Entrants and win success by first becoming a mechanic.

THE NON-TECHNICAL JOBS

Not all who join the Royal Air Force are mechanically minded; nor does the R.A.F. expect them to be. There are many non-technical jobs to be done, and plenty of opportunities for those men and women whose interests and inclinations lie in quite different directions. There are, among others, jobs for clerks of various

181

grades, for draughtsmen, bricklayers, cooks, coxswains and other
motor-boat crew, dental mechanics, dispensers, laboratory assistants,
nursing orderlies, photographers, plumbers, physical training instructors, police, tailors, telephonists, air traffic control assistants, and
motor cyclists. These are but a few of the non-technical trades
open to those who would like to join the R.A.F., but whose aptitude
for things mechanical is not highly developed.

For lads who have no aptitude for mechanical things, but who
want to join the Royal Air Force, there is a special scheme of training
under which they qualify as general clerks, accounting clerks or
equipment assistants. The boys join between the ages of 16 and $17\frac{1}{2}$
and are known as Administrative Apprentices. Their training lasts
about sixteen months and is followed by a further eight months'
training at an R.A.F. unit. They have the same facilities for sport,
games, recreation and hobbies as Aircraft Apprentices and Boy
Entrants and, like them, receive pay while under training. In
addition, they are, like the others, fed, clothed and housed and given
any medical attention they may need—all for nothing. Their general
education is also continued, and everything is done to encourage
them to broaden their interests to embrace matters other than those
connected with their training and the R.A.F. The rank they get
on completing their apprenticeship depends upon the marks they get
in their final examinations. If they do well, they are at once promoted
to Aircraftman First-Class; otherwise they change from Apprentice
to Aircraftman Second-Class and start their career in the lowest
rank. Normally, they sign on for twelve years' regular service, but
may apply for re-engagement to complete further regular service for
a pension.

After a year or two, they may have the chance of a commission
in the Secretarial or Equipment Branches of the Royal Air Force or
may be selected for aircrew duty. Those who become pilots or
navigators will, if fit, remain pilots or navigators until their twelve
years' regular service expires, but will be eligible to re-engage to
complete twenty-two years' service for "aircrew pension." They also
stand a chance of winning a commission as a pilot or navigator.

For many years the R.A.F. classified its different " trades " by
groups, all trades carrying the same rates of pay being in the same
group. The most skilled and the highest paid were in Group " A ";
those needing less skill and commanding less pay being, according

TENDING THE R.A.F.'s WARPLANES

AN INSTRUMENT REPAIRER CHECKING THE ACCURACY OF A D.R. COMPASS.

to their rating, in Groups "B," "C," and "D." Soon after the end of the Second World War, because of the growing technical complexity and intricacy of warplanes and their equipment, it became obvious that classifying the various trades by groups on a pay basis was becoming unsatisfactory. A conference was therefore held on the matter, and as a result of it a new and better scheme was introduced. This not only raised the standard of skill of "tradesmen" but provided new inducements and incentives for airmen and airwomen to seek promotion and to make the R.A.F. a life career. Previously, there had been only one channel of promotion—through the non-commissioned ranks. This meant that promotion was limited by the R.A.F.'s need of N.C.O.s. In peacetime, a skilled technician might remain in the same rank for several years, his way blocked because there were no vacancies in his trade in ranks higher than that which he held.

Now, airmen and airwomen have a double channel of promotion.

TENDING THE R.A.F.'s WARPLANES

CHECKING OVER AND ADJUSTING AN AIR CAMERA.

They can climb the old ladder, or the new one. The new scheme created four additional ranks, known as Junior Technician (with a status corresponding to that of a Leading Aircraftman), Corporal Technician (with the status of Corporal), Senior Technician (with the status of Sergeant), and Chief Technician (with the status of Flight Sergeant), each higher rank carrying a higher rate of pay. An extra rung was also added to the old ladder in the form of a new rank —that of Senior Aircraftman, coming between Leading Aircraftman and Corporal.

Special "stripes," worn inverted, were devised for the new technician ranks. The Junior Technician has a single stripe, the Corporal two, the Senior Technician three, and the Chief Technician three surmounted by a crown. The Senior Aircraftman wears a three-bladed " prop " badge, to distinguish him from the Leading Aircraftman, who wears a two-bladed propeller badge. The two lower ranks (Aircraftman 2 and Aircraftman 1) carry no badge of any kind. Under the old order, N.C.O.s had to display qualities of leadership, be ready to accept responsibility and capable of enforcing discipline. Skilled men not suitable by disposition or temperament for leadership and responsibility will now gain promotion via the technician ranks, in which these qualities are not demanded or even expected.

To simplify matters, the one hundred or so existing trades were embodied in twenty-two trade groups as follows :

1. Aircraft Engineering.
2. Radio Engineering.
3. Armament Engineering.
4. Electrical and Instrument Engineering.
5. General Engineering.
6. Mechanical Transport.
7. Marine Craft.
8. Airfield Construction.
9. Air Traffic Control and Fire Fighting.
10. General Service.
11. Ground Signalling.
12. Radar Operating.
13. Safety and Surface.
14. Photography.
15. Medical.
16. Dental.
17. Accounting and Secretarial.
18. Supply.
19. Catering.
20. Police.
21. Music.
22. R.A.F. Regiment.

[*Crown Copyright Reserved.*

AN ARMOURER REFILLS THE AMMUNITION BOXES OF A VAMPIRE JET FIGHTER.

[*Central Press.*

A WAR-TIME PICTURE OF A TORPEDO ABOUT TO BE LOADED INTO A COASTAL
COMMAND BEAUFORT.

In most of these trade groups there are Advanced Trades, corresponding broadly to the original Group " A " trades ; Skilled Trades, corresponding broadly to the original Groups " B " and " C " trades ; and " Trade Assistants "—those classified as unskilled or semi-skilled.

Trained men entering the R.A.F. from civil life and able to pass a trade test for any aircraftman rank up to and including Junior Technician are given that rank and paid accordingly. Those who enter untrained start to learn their trade as soon as they have finished their recruits' training. Some take a course of basic training at a properly equipped school ; others go to a squadron or unit and acquire skill " on the job," being closely supervised at first. The recruit who goes to the school is promoted to Aircraftman 1 as soon as he passes the school examinations ; those who go straight to the job are promoted to A.C.1 as soon as they can do their job without supervision. In any case, an A.C.2 is promoted to A.C.1 after $1\frac{1}{2}$ years in the rank regardless of examinations or progress. While under training airmen and airwomen are classed as Trade Assistants.

TENDING THE R.A.F.'s WARPLANES

Promotion thereafter depends largely upon the efforts of the individual. All possible help is offered by the R.A.F., and those who are prepared to serve for ten years or more are encouraged to take advanced training in order to make themselves specialists in the trade of their choice or that to which they have been allocated. The new scheme did away with several anomalies which had deterred some airmen from seeking promotion and advancement. It could happen, for instance, that a Leading Aircraftman would lose his rank when he "remustered" to a higher trade group, because it was seldom possible for anyone to pass the examination with high enough marks to hold the rank of L.A.C., even if there were vacancies in that rank and trade. If, after getting his "props" back, the same airman remustered to a still higher group, he might well again lose the rank and become an A.C.2 or A.C.1. Both times he would have suffered loss of pay. This sort of thing cannot happen now. Under the revised scheme promotion and advancement are continuous; there is no risk of "slipping down the ladder" as in the past.

[*Central Press.*]

ARMOURERS LOADING A TWIN-ENGINED BOMBER, WHILE FITTERS CHECK
ENGINES AND LANDING GEAR.

IN THE ANTE-ROOM OF AN OFFICERS' MESS.

COMMISSIONS IN THE R.A.F.

COMMISSIONS in the Royal Air Force are easier to get to-day than ever before. Standards have not been lowered, but more doors have been opened. At one time, nearly all the officer vacancies were filled by qualified pilots and navigators. These still fill all the appointments calling for flying and navigational knowledge and experience, but the organization of the Royal Air Force has grown so complex that there are hundreds of vacancies for officers which can be filled by those without flying experience.

" Operational " pilots and navigators go into the General Duties Branch when they are commissioned, and hold either a short service or a permanent commission. The short service commission runs for a specified period of years—usually eight—and is followed by a period of service on the reserve. A permanent commission offers its holder a career in the Royal Air Force and a pension at the end of it. The length of time served depends upon rank and age ; the higher the rank the later the retiring age and the bigger the pension. Holders of short service commissions are often given permanent commissions. On the other hand, hundreds of young men take a short service commission with the sole object of gaining valuable flying experience and, when the short service commission expires, of turning to commercial aviation.

A large proportion of those who are granted permanent commissions in the Royal Air Force first go to the R.A.F. College, Cranwell, as cadets. Here they receive a three-year course of training which not only includes instruction in flying and all its associated subjects, but embraces, too, studies normally taken at universities. Cranwell is, in effect, an Air University and those who pass through it have every prospect of an interesting career before them when, as qualified pilots, they say good-bye to classroom lectures and instructional flying and set out for their first squadron appointment.

Candidates for cadetships are chosen with great care. This is

[*Keystone.*

PASSING-OUT INSPECTION AT AN R.A.F. STATION.

only natural because upon them will fall heavy responsibilities in later years. They have to be young, well educated and very fit, intelligent and quick-witted and endowed with all the qualities which are looked for in a leader. Most cadets go to Cranwell from civil life, but some are drawn from R.A.F. Aircraft Apprentices who distinguish themselves during their technical training. Permanent commissions are also given to university graduates, usually to those who have served with a university air squadron—although this is not an indispensable condition.

It would be impossible for every pilot and navigator to enter the Royal Air Force through Cranwell, but as the Air Ministry likes as many as possible of its pilots and navigators to hold a commission it grants a short service commission (for eight years) to all who are accepted for training and pass a preliminary ground training course. The commission is in the rank of acting pilot officer on probation, and is confirmed (and the holder promoted to the rank of pilot officer) when the full flying and ground courses of

[*Crown Copyright Reserved.*

THE INSTRUCTOR "LISTENS IN" WHILE HIS PUPILS PRACTISE THE ARTS OF DISCUSSION AND DEBATE.

COMMISSIONS IN THE R.A.F.

[*Graphic Photo Union.*

PUPIL PILOTS AT THE R.A.F. COLLEGE ARE SHOWN THE CORRECT WAY FOR LANDING.

training are completed and the candidate has shown that he has the qualities of character looked for in an officer. Those whose commissions are not confirmed serve as N.C.O. pilots or navigators but become eligible for a short service commission later if they reach the required standard. Many of those whose commissions are confirmed at the end of the training period are given permanent commissions, like those who pass through Cranwell.

Most young men are interested chiefly in the General Duties Branch because their inclinations and ambitions lie only in flying and navigating. But if for any reason—say a slight defect in vision —they are unable to qualify for the General Duties Branch, and possess engineering skill, they can apply for a commission in the Technical Branch. If they are successful they almost invariably receive a permanent commission. Many permanent commissions in the Technical Branch also go to airmen who have completed a certain period as " tradesmen " in one of the several groups in which trades calling for the highest skill are found. Most of them are former Aircraft Apprentices.

RANK DISTINCTIONS IN THE
ROYAL AIR FORCE

Key to Coloured Plate

1. Marshal of the Royal Air Force
2. Air Chief Marshal . . . Cap : "Patent Leather" peak with gold oak
3. Air Marshal . . . . leaves ; sleeves and shoulder-straps varying
4. Air Vice-Marshal . . . as shown in plate.
5. Air Commodore . . .
6. Group Captain . . . Cap : "Patent Leather" peak with one row of gold oak leaves.

7. Wing Commander . . .
8. Squadron Leader . . .
9. Flight Lieutenant . . . Cap : cloth peak ; sleeves and shoulder-straps
10. Flying Officer. . . . varying as shown in plate.
11. Pilot Officer . . . .
12. Wing Commander's Cap and all other Officers.
13. Officer's Beret.
14. Navigator's Badge.
15. Pilot's Badge.
16. Signaller's Badge.
17. Wireless Operator's Badge.
18. P.T. Instructor's Badge.
19. R.A.F. Apprentice's Cap (Cranwell C Squadron)
20. Distinguished Flying Cross.
21. Distinguished Flying Medal.
22. Air Force Medal.
23. Air Force Cross.
A. Greatcoat Shoulder Rank Distinctions.
B. Officer's Uniform Sleeve Distinctions.

RANK EQUIVALENTS IN THE R.A.F., NAVY AND ARMY

Marshal of the Royal Air Force = Admiral of the Fleet or Field-Marshal.
Air Chief Marshal = Admiral or General.
Air Marshal = Vice-Admiral or Lieut.-General.
Air Vice-Marshal = Rear-Admiral or Major-General.
Air Commodore = Commodore or Brigadier.
Group Captain = Captain or Colonel.
Wing Commander = Commander or Lieut.-Colonel.
Squadron Leader = Lieut.-Commander or Major.
Flight Lieutenant = Lieutenant or Captain.
Flying Officer = Sub-Lieutenant or Lieutenant.
Pilot Officer = Midshipman and Warrant Officer or Second Lieutenant.

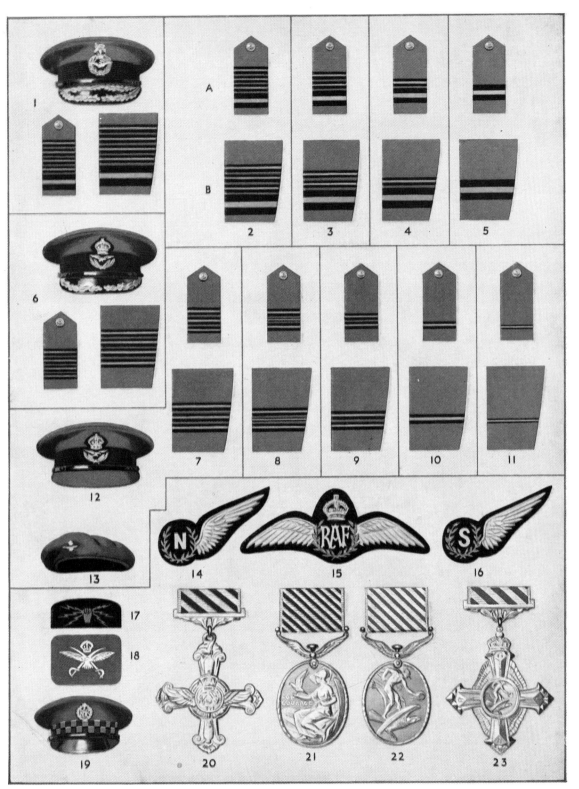

COMMISSIONS IN THE R.A.F.

Technical Branch officers at first specialize in one of three subjects: Armaments, Engineering and Signalling. As they grow older and assume greater responsibility they broaden their knowledge until they are experts on all technical matters, and are qualified to hold the most responsible appointments available to officers of this branch.

Those who are medically fit and of the right temperament can take a course of flying training, but this does not involve their transfer to the General Duties Branch or to an operational squadron.

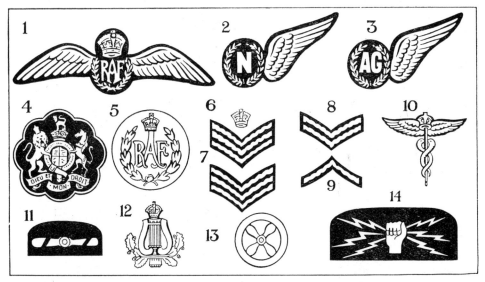

1. Qualified Pilot's Wings.   2. Navigator.   3. Air Gunner.   4. Warrant Officer.   5. R.A.F. Cap Badge. 6. Flight Sergeant. 7. Sergeant. 8. Corporal. 9. Good Conduct Stripe. 10. Medical Officer's Collar Badge. 11. Leading Aircraftman. 12. Central Bandsman. 13. Apprentice. 14. Wireless Operator.

Those who are considered unsuitable for flying training are not penalized in any way. A number of Technical Branch officers come into the R.A.F. from the universities.

Altogether, there are sixteen different branches in the Royal Air Force in which commissions are granted. Several of them call for training of a kind which the Royal Air Force does not give, and those who enter these branches have first to get the necessary degrees in the recognized manner. This applies to the Medical, Dental, Legal and Chaplains Branches and to some extent to the Airfield Construction Branch, whose duty it is to see that the R.A.F.'s mobility is not hampered by lack of operating facilities wherever it is in action. Its officers have to be trained civil engineers or skilled in the operation of electric power plant, pumping plant, and similar essential services.

Educational Branch officers are the R.A.F.'s school-teachers, who meet the needs of those wishing to improve their knowledge of a subject for the purpose of gaining promotion, preparing for civil life, or merely for pleasure. The Provost Branch supplies the police, who not only keep an eye on airmen on and off the " station," but also see that the security regulations which safeguard the R.A.F.'s secrets are enforced.

Officers of the Catering Branch plan the meals and look after food supplies, and those of the Physical Training Branch arrange the P.T. parades and organize sports and games. In the Marine Branch are the R.A.F.'s " naval " officers, who have charge of the numerous marine vessels which form a little navy of their own : launches for use at flying-boat bases and coastal bombing ranges ; target and torpedo recovery ships; target towing and rescue craft; and flying-boat depot ships.

By courtesy of] *[" Flight."*

AN INSTRUCTOR IN AERODYNAMICS USES A WIND TUNNEL TO DEMONSTRATE AIR FLOW OVER THE WINGS OF AN AEROPLANE.

[Crown Copyright Reserved.

THIS ORDERLY ROOM SCENE FORMS PART OF THE TRAINING GIVEN TO THOSE ABOUT TO BE COMMISSIONED.

Fighter Control officers guide defensive fighters by radio to the vicinity of airborne raiders, using information gleaned from their radar screens. With bombers now flying at 600 miles an hour—10 miles a minute—very precise direction for the fighters is needed, or they will miss the raider. There will be little chance of a second attempt at interception, and far less satisfaction comes from shooting down a raider on its return from bombing a target than comes from shooting it down on the way to it.

Equipment Branch officers have to take care of something like 800,000 items of stores and equipment which the R.A.F. needs for its everyday work. These items range from nuts and bolts to big jet-propelled bombers, and they all have to pass through the hands of Equipment officers at one time or another. The Secretarial Branch handles matters relating to the pay and allowances of officers and airmen and deals with other kinds of accountancy.

Finally, there is the R.A.F. Regiment, which was formed during the war to defend R.A.F. airfields against ground and low-flying attack by the enemy. Squadrons—particularly fighter squadrons co-operating with the Army—have to work as far forward as possible and are therefore frequently within easy reach of enemy air attack and sometimes artillery fire. The R.A.F. Regiment not only provides trained men for the defence of airfields; it also ensures that the airmen on the squadron can provide trained reinforcements.

Permanent commissions are given to officers in all branches except that of Airfield Construction. Short service commissions are available in all branches except the Marine and Legal Branches; only a few S.S.C.s go to the Technical Branch.

While the National Service Act is in force, two kinds of National Service commission are being awarded—one under Scheme A and the other under Scheme B. These National Service commissions are designed to encourage their holders to make a longer stay in the Royal Air Force than the statutory period of their National Service —some lead to permanent commissions and an R.A.F. career—or to accept service in the Royal Auxiliary Air Force or the Royal Air Force Volunteer Reserve when their National Service period ends. Both schemes are attractive and often make a strong appeal to those who did not previously realize the opportunities which the R.A.F. offers.

CENTRAL BAND OF THE R.A.F. ON PARADE IN CEREMONIAL DRESS.

[*P.A. Reuter Photo.*

Members of the Women's Royal Auxiliary Air Force arriving at an R.A.F. station for a week-end training exercise in detecting and plotting hostile aircraft.

THE WOMEN'S ROYAL AIR FORCE

MANY parents are surprised when a daughter shows interest in aeroplanes. They ought not to be. From the very dawn of flying women have been active in its advancement, sharing its joys and running its risks. Women flew in balloons more than a hundred years ago. They were among the earliest to " venture aloft " in aeroplanes ; some of the most skilful pilots of the pioneering days were women. Some set up aviation businesses ; some became flying instructresses, some engineers, some mechanics. They have invaded almost every branch of the aeronautical profession.

There is more scope to-day for airminded women than ever before. Some of the best opportunities for them are to be found in the Women's Royal Air Force. In its range of " trades " the W.R.A.F. offers an opening to almost everyone whose first interest lies with flying—except as members of an aeroplane's crew ! The flight deck is still territory forbidden to women of the W.R.A.F., but those who believe that the cockpit, the navigator's, the signaller's and flight engineer's stations should be thrown open to women can take heart. Qualified women pilots are, even now, accepted for the W.R.A.F. Volunteer Reserve ; that may be the thin end of a very welcome wedge.

Women first served side by side with men in the R.A.F. in World War I. In fact, the first W.R.A.F. was formed on the same day that the R.A.F. was formed—1st April, 1918. When the war ended in November of that year, the W.R.A.F. had 25,000 members, whose services had been so valuable that the Government had every intention of putting the W.R.A.F. on a permanent basis. Alas for plans ! After the war the country started to spend more than it could afford, and one of the economies decided upon was the disbanding of the W.R.A.F. By March, 1922, all its members had been demobilized. But the part which women had played added another chapter to the glorious story of the R.A.F., and when war clouds began to gather over Europe again that part was remembered and steps were taken to re-create a special women's service to help the R.A.F. once more.

As a measure of economy, the Government tried to meet the need by forming air companies within the Auxiliary Territorial Service (formed in 1938), but experience proved this to be false economy and in 1939 the Women's Auxiliary Air Force was formed. The title suggested that the W.A.A.F. would have only a temporary existence. This time the circumstances of World War I were reversed. A year or so after World War II, the temporary W.A.A.F. changed its name and its status and became the permanent W.R.A.F. So much for history.

The W.R.A.F. is an extremely important branch of the Royal Air Force and its members increase the number of skilled " trades-men " available. Most of the W.R.A.F. trades are " technical " and have a direct bearing upon the airworthiness, battleworthiness and efficiency of aeroplanes and their engines. The women have to undergo the same training and pass the same tests as the men before they can be employed at their trade, but the courses of instruction give those who take them every chance of succeeding. There are no concessions for women. That is only right and proper ;

The plotting table in an Operations Room showing the positions of " hostile " aircraft during an air exercise. The plotters wear headphones and move the indicators to accord with information reaching them from observation posts.

most jobs in the R.A.F. set their own standards of skill and efficiency, and cannot be entrusted to the inadequately trained.

One does not have to wonder long why standards are high. An aeroplane is a complex piece of machinery made up of thousands of parts. It is, as was mentioned in an earlier chapter, an assembly of mechanical and electrical items that form a nervous system almost as sensitive as that of a living body. It is robust and capable of taking hard knocks, but it is always waging a war—not on a visible enemy but upon " gravity," that unseen force which, given the smallest chance, will bring the aeroplane down from the sky as swiftly as will a shell or bullet. Work that is below the minimum standard ; carelessness, ignorance, inattention—any of these can give gravity its opportunity.

This need for skill, care, knowledge and attention makes the work of the W.R.A.F. more exacting but doubles its interest, and one seldom hears the complaint : " I'm bored with this job ;

it's so monotonous." You can never be bored with a job that demands unremitting care and attention. There is, too, a wide variety in the jobs offered by the W.R.A.F.

In 1939, the W.A.A.F. had only six trades : cooks, clerks, mess and kitchen orderlies, equipment assistants, M.T. drivers, and fabric workers, in addition to a sprinkling of administrative officers. At the end of 1943, when its strength stood at 182,000, including 5,788 officers, the W.A.A.F. had a list of no fewer than 83 different trades, most of which had their counterparts in the R.A.F. This meant that every member of the W.A.A.F. serving in such trades was a direct substitute for an R.A.F. man and that the R.A.F. was that much stronger in consequence. Seventy per cent of all W.A.A.F. airwomen were employed in technical trades at that time. To-day, there are only slightly fewer than in the peak months of the war.

Recruits, regardless of trade group, get the same pay until they complete their training.

Opportunities for promotion are good, and women can, like men, transfer to a higher paid trade if they can prove that they are competent and can pass the examination.

As members of the W.A.A.F. shared its work during the war so they shared some of the R.A.F.'s dangers. The bravery, courage, heroism, gallantry and devotion to duty shown by members of the W.A.A.F. in World War II wrote a bright chapter in the glowing history of the British Armed Forces. A hundred honours and awards, including a

[Crown Copyright Reserved.

AN AIRWOMAN FITTER ASSISTS WITH THE SERVICING OF THE ENGINES OF A JET FIGHTER.

THE WOMEN'S ROYAL AIR FORCE

[*Crown Copyright Reserved.*

AT THIS STATION EACH AIRMAN IS SERVED INDIVIDUALLY IN THE DINING HALL.

George Cross and thousands of " Mentioned in Dispatches," rewarded and recorded deeds more valiant than anything called for by the dictates of duty. Time after time, members of the W.A.A.F. stayed at their posts in imminent peril of their lives in order that a vital service should not be interrupted. Time after time, regardless of personal danger, they risked their lives to save the lives of others.

Nor is that all. Many members of the W.A.A.F. volunteered to serve with " underground " groups in the enemy-occupied countries. They were taught the arts of the *saboteur,* or trained in the use of wireless, given false identity papers and dropped by parachute to make contact with the leaders of the resistance movements to which they had been assigned. This was work of the most dangerous kind. If caught they faced almost certain death, or hours of torture. They knew it, and were not afraid.

Let citations accompanying awards for gallantry tell some of the stories. Because space cannot be found here for more than a few, the names of the principal characters in these dramatic events are left out ; there are so many others which deserve inclusion.

*   *   *   *   *

"At 0100 hours, an aeroplane crashed near the W.A.A.F. quarters, the pilot being seriously injured, another officer killed outright, and two airmen slightly injured. Upon hearing the crash, Corporal P—— (later commissioned) rushed out to it and, although the aircraft was burning and she knew that there were bombs on board, she stood on the wreckage, roused the pilot, who was stunned, and assisted him in getting clear, releasing his parachute harness in doing so. When he was on the ground and about thirty yards away, a 120-lb. bomb went off.

Corporal P—— at once threw herself on top of the pilot to protect him from blast. Her prompt and courageous action undoubtedly helped to save the pilot's life."

*   *   *   *   *

"On 18th August, 1940, during a heavy bombing attack on Biggin Hill aerodrome, Sergeant M—— manned the telephone linking the defence posts as well as being in charge of the dispatch

[*Crown Copyright Reserved.*

AIRMEN AND AIRWOMEN STUDY INDUSTRIAL GEOGRAPHY.

INSTRUCTING AIRMEN AND AIRWOMEN IN RADAR.

of the ammunition required. A large amount of ammunition was stored near her office, but Sergeant M—— remained at her post, giving words of encouragement to the airmen near. This airwoman displayed exceptional courage and coolness, which had a great moral effect on all those with whom she came in contact. As soon as bombs stopped falling and long before the ' All Clear ' was sounded, this airwoman was marking unexploded bomb craters by means of red flags."

*   *   *   *   *

" During a heavy bombing attack on an aerodrome, Sergeant T—— was the operator on duty in the telephone exchange in the Operations Room building. Bombs were falling all around the building but this airwoman displayed great coolness, despite the knowledge that there was no overhead protection. The Operations Room eventually received a direct hit and caught fire, but Sergeant T—— remained at her post and maintained communications until they were cut off and she was ordered to a shelter trench."

*   *   *   *   *

"A Wellington bomber crashed and burst into flames. Corporal H—— ran to the aeroplane in spite of the fact that the fuel tanks had exploded. She heard cries for help and found the rear gunner trapped in his turret, surrounded by flames and with his clothing and harness on fire.

"Corporal H—— managed to get the escape hatch open, but the gunner was unable to make his way out. Corporal H—— helped the gunner and assisted him to an ambulance. But for her gallant action, the gunner would have lost his life."

* * * * *

"Leading Aircraftwoman L. S. E—— was in charge of a balloon site at Cardiff which was attacked by enemy aircraft. Despite the intensity of the attack, this airwoman supervised the balloon operation

[Crown Copyright Reserved.

THE ROYAL AUXILIARY AIR FORCE.

Spare-time Servicewomen of a R.Aux.A.F. Fighter Control Unit plotting and recording during an air exercise.

Lunch-time for W.R.A.F. Officer Cadets, who undergo a three months' course of training before being commissioned.

and ensured its completion. The site was later hit by a bomb, and three members of the balloon crew were killed and four wounded. Leading Aircraftwoman E—— was severely hurt, but took charge of the situation. She maintained the balloon in its operational position until assistance arrived. She undoubtedly saved the life of at least one airwoman who might have died without first-aid treatment. She showed outstanding leadership, coolness and courage."

*   *   *   *   *

"Flight Officer (Honorary) C. P. W—— was parachuted into France on 23rd September, 1943, as courier to a powerful circuit in south-western France and as liaison officer with a resistance group numbering 1,000 men commanded by a French colonel. Flight Officer W—— established excellent relations with the commander and played a large part in organizing and developing the group."

*   *   *   *   *

" Flight Officer (Honorary) B. Y. C—— parachuted into south-west France in August, 1943, as a W/T operator. She proved to be one of the most technically efficient wireless operators sent to the field and, maintaining her high standard throughout her service of over a year, she sent about 400 messages without detection. This work played a large part in establishing one of the most powerful circuits in France and enabled 140 successful drop operations to be carried out. In order to avoid D/F detection by the enemy, Flight Officer C—— never transmitted twice in the same place. During the whole of her time in the field she always showed complete devotion to duty and abnegation of self. At the battle of Castelnau she carried her radio set through German lines under fire and got through to home stations from a roadside farmhouse. At the battle of Lannemaizen she showed great courage and devotion to duty under machine-gunning from the air."

*   *   *   *   *

" Section Officer (Honorary) M. O'S—— was dropped in France on 22nd March, 1944, as wireless operator to a resistance group in the Limoges area. Though handicapped through imperfect technical knowledge and the consequence of a serious illness she nevertheless, by patience, perseverance and devotion to duty, made a success of her work. In two months she became a first-class and fully reliable operator. In addition to cycling some 50 kilometres every day collecting and delivering messages and in spite of the great amount of traffic she had to handle she found time to train three local operators. She lived most of the time in conditions of unusual squalor, without complaining, and it was due in large measure to her persistent efforts and untiring devotion that the circuit achieved its success."

*   *   *   *   *

By deeds like these, and by their unswerving loyalty, the members of the war-time W.A.A.F. covered themselves with a glory as bright as that which covers the Service to which they are affiliated. Their mantle falls upon all those who join the W.R.A.F. in peace-time.

CADETS OF THE A.T.C. AT SUMMER CAMP AWAITING THEIR TURN TO FLY.

BACKING UP THE "REGULARS"

EACH of the Armed Services is supported in peace-time and strengthened in war by its reservists. The Royal Air Force is "backed" by its General Reserve, by the Royal Auxiliary Air Force, the Royal Air Force Volunteer Reserve, University Air Squadrons and, in a different way, by the Air Training Corps. The reservists of the Women's Royal Air Force are found by the Women's Royal Auxiliary Air Force and Women's Royal Air Force Volunteer Reserve.

At the outbreak of war the intensity of work immediately increases, and a large reserve of trained men is necessary so that existing Royal Air Force units can be expanded from peace-time to war-time size swiftly and smoothly. This need is partly covered by ex-regular and National Service airmen who have a reserve liability to meet after they return to civil life. During their period of reserve liability (which is normally about four years) reservists have to undergo spare-time training, both to refresh their skill and to receive instruction on new equipment and in new techniques. The actual training required varies according to circumstances. Those whose civilian employment is the same as that of their R.A.F. job often do no reserve training.

The National Serviceman's reserve liability has been set by Parliament at sixty days, spread over four years, with not more than twenty-one days in any one year. This liability may be met by service in the R.Aux.A.F., or the R.A.F.V.R. which provide valuable opportunities for the training of pilots, navigators and other flying men, as well as for those in the more highly skilled branches.

THE ROYAL AUXILIARY AIR FORCE

This consists of units which form part of the front line of the Royal Air Force, and which are trained to front-line standard.

A ROYAL AUXILIARY AIR FORCE VAMPIRE BEING RE-ARMED, RE-FUELLED AND SERVICED AFTER AIR EXERCISE.

By courtesy of]   [*The de Havilland Aircraft Co., Ltd.*

DE HAVILLAND VENOM HIGH-ALTITUDE JET INTERCEPTOR FIGHTER.

The vapour trail is symbolic of its great climbing powers.

BACKING UP THE "REGULARS"

[*Photographic News Agencies, Ltd.*

THE QUEEN MOTHER INSPECTING MEN OF THE 600 (CITY OF LONDON) SQUADRON,
ROYAL AUXILIARY AIR FORCE, OF WHICH SHE IS HONORARY AIR COMMODORE.

These units are organized and operate on a part-time basis in peace-time, and come into full operation as soon as an "emergency" arises. They are raised and maintained on a county or city basis by the Territorial and Auxiliary Forces Association in the same way as are units of the Territorial Army; the same applies to the Women's Royal Auxiliary Air Force.

R.Aux.A.F. units are commanded by an Auxiliary Air Force officer, and are manned mainly by other officers and airmen of the Royal Auxiliary Air Force and partly by a "core" of regular officers and airmen who act as instructors. The units are of four distinct types:

(*a*) Flying Squadrons armed with fighter aircraft.

(*b*) Fighter Control Units, whose function is to train the operators and technicians who will man the United Kingdom defence control and reporting system on mobilization. They provide a reserve of highly skilled men and women who are employed on duties varying from that of officers who control the movement of fighters to radar mechanics, radar operators, teleprinter operators and aircraft plotters.

(*c*) Light Anti-Aircraft Regiment Squadrons, to provide for the close anti-aircraft defence of airfields.

(*d*) Air Observation Post Squadrons, whose job is to control and direct the fire of artillery and to undertake photographic reconnaissance. The pilots are Territorial Army officers of the Royal Artillery; aircraft maintenance is looked after by men of the Royal Auxiliary Air Force.

Royal Air Force Volunteer Reserve

The purpose of the Royal Air Force Volunteer Reserve is to provide a reserve of trained officers, airmen and airwomen in both flying and ground duties. It is open to volunteers who undergo

A RADIO STATION MANNED BY TWO CORPORALS OF THE AIR TRAINING CORPS.

[*H. Taylor.*

Air Training Corps cadets in the Link Trainer Room at an R.A.F. station. Duplicate instruments and the " crab " are seen on the instructor's table.

spare-time training and come up for full-time service with the Royal Air Force if a state of war or similar emergency exists. Generally speaking, those admitted to the R.A.F.V.R. are trained men or women who have had previous service in the R.A.F. or W.A.A.F., but others may also apply to join. Flying training is given at Reserve Flying Schools ; other training is given at Reserve Centres and R.A.F. Stations. The training is designed to keep officers, aircrew and tradesmen efficient and up to date in their knowledge.

University Air Squadrons

The purpose of the University Air Squadrons (which form part of the R.A.F.V.R.) is to give training during their university career to those who wish to prepare themselves for commissioned service in the regular, auxiliary or reserve R.A.F. The squadrons are also designed to promote in the universities an interest in flying and its associated problems and to maintain a liaison with the Universities in the technical and research branches of aviation.

BACKING UP THE "REGULARS"

THE AIR TRAINING CORPS

The aims of the Air Training Corps are to encourage among young men a practical interest in aviation, and by training to fit them to serve their country in the Royal Air Force, its auxiliaries and reserves, or in the Air Branch of the Royal Navy. The organization also helps to promote healthy sports and pastimes, to foster a spirit of adventure and to cultivate the qualities of mind and body which go to the making of a leader and a good citizen.

Cadets who obtain the Air Training Corps Proficiency Certificate have special opportunities for entry into the Royal Air Force, including entry as officers through the Royal Air Force College, Cranwell, or by way of the aircraft apprenticeship training schemes. Proficient cadets who pass the tests may also be given aircrew training in their period of National Service, or before, by winning a scholarship entitling them to learn to fly at an approved flying club.

The Corps is organized in wings, usually on a county basis, and may consist of any number of squadrons formed by schools or

[*Crown Copyright Reserved.*

Members of a Fighter Control Unit of the Royal Auxiliary Air Force taking part in an exercise during their
summer camp at an R.A.F. station.

[*Graphic Photo Union.*

DE HAVILLAND CHIPMUNK TRAINERS REPLACE TIGER MOTHS AT OXFORD UNIVERSITY AIR
SQUADRON.

communities.   A number of schools which previously had Air Training Corps Units have now joined the Combined Cadet Force and
their R.A.F. sections are separate from the Air Training Corps as such.

The Air Training Corps was formed in February, 1941.   It
was superimposed, as it were, upon an earlier organization of a very
similar character, the Air Defence Cadet Corps, which was another
" invention " of the Air League of the British Empire.   The Air
League felt that thousands of boys up and down the country would
be only too glad to enrol in an organization devoted to the study
and practice of aeronautics, even in an elementary form.   Money
was raised, the help of prominent local citizens was enlisted, and
within a few months of the scheme's being launched squadrons
were taking shape and filling up fast.

In the early days, the boys and their officers had to be content
with the roughest of instructional material and the least satisfactory
kind of accommodation, but keenness overcame all difficulties and
by the time war broke out the A.D.C.C. was firmly established and
one of the recognized institutions of British aeronautical life.   When
the A.T.C. was created, the Air Ministry had a complete working

organization already in being to take over. Thousands of A.D.C.C. and A.T.C. cadets joined the Royal Air Force and the Fleet Air Arm during the war, and many won heroic distinctions—including one Victoria Cross.

The experience of the last war confirmed the wisdom of the decision to entrust to the Auxiliaries and Reserve a large share in the air defence of the United Kingdom. The success of the Royal Auxiliary Air Force squadrons in the Battle of Britain was in itself a justification of that policy. To-day, these Forces must bear an even heavier burden ; the whole of the country's defence system rests on the joint support of the regular and auxiliary forces, and for the latter to attain the set standard of efficiency an even more rigorous and often more complex course of training is necessary.

The branches of the Reserve do more than strengthen the Royal Air Force. They satisfy the needs and desires of hundreds of men, women and young people who, for a variety of reasons, cannot or do not wish to join the regular Royal Air Force and Women's Royal Air Force. Motives for joining the Reserve vary. Some volunteers find the technical trade of their choice an interesting hobby ; some are anxious to serve their country and are not set upon learning one particular trade or employment ; some seek to turn the training they receive to personal advantage in order that they may secure a more congenial job in civil life ; others join in order to share the social life and close comradeship that are inseparable from the communities which the various units create.

For all but the general reservists, training goes on throughout the year, but the culminating point of the year's work is the annual " camp." This is usually arranged during the summer so that those who cannot get extra time off may make the occasion their holiday. The camp is usually held at an R.A.F. station, and the reservists live, work and train very much as do the " regulars." It is almost as though they had been mobilized.

A.T.C. cadets, too, have their annual camps, also at R.A.F. stations. The stations most often chosen for them are those which can offer the excitements and thrills of flying in a warplane, and never were there keener " aircrew " than these eager youngsters. Most of them have the ambition to wear one of the R.A.F.'s flying badges later on, and for them the annual camp cannot come round too quickly or last too long.

A GLOSTER METEOR 8 JET FIGHTER POWERED WITH 2 ARMSTRONG SIDDELEY SAPPHIRE
AXIAL-FLOW ENGINES.

THE R.A.F.
IN WAR AND PEACE

BECAUSE the Royal Air Force is our first line of defence this does
not mean that it merely has to guard our shores and drive off any
hostile forces that try to invade us by land, sea or air. " Offence is
the best form of defence " and " Strike to defend " are old and true
sayings and much of the R.A.F.'s work is therefore offensive. In the
event of war, Bomber Command at once seeks out targets in the
enemy's own country. It goes for airfields, aircraft and other war
factories, oil storage depots, railway junctions, canals, power stations,
dams, submarine pens, docks, harbours, ships at sea—any object, in
fact, that helps the enemy to wage war on us and is within its range.

For the defence of these islands from air attack we look primarily
to Fighter Command, backed by a powerful and interlocking system
of radar, searchlight and anti-aircraft organizations. Besides defending our shores, Fighter Command protects coastal shipping, lends a

hand to the Army in land battles, and harasses the enemy wherever it can reach him—as it did in World War II when it began those daring " sweeps " across the Channel late in 1940, which, as time went on, grew bigger and bigger until Fighter Command was more occupied with offensive than defensive tasks.

Coastal Command also has a dual role of offence and defence in protecting our shipping. Our maritime lines of communication are more important to us in war than anything else. We cannot grow enough food to feed ourselves ; more has to be brought in and the bulk of it must come by sea. Nor do we produce all the vital materials we need to make weapons of war, nor the fuel for our warplanes, tanks, lorries, mobile generating plant, oil-burning ships, farm tractors, and all the thousands of other internal combustion engines that must be kept going if victory is to be ours. All these things have to come to us from other lands. Coastal Command, therefore, has a task no less heavy and responsible than that of Fighter or Bomber Command. Working closely with the Royal Navy, and under the direction of the Admiralty, Coastal Command sets up new bases at home and abroad so that its flying-boats and landplanes can strike the most telling blows against the enemy's submarines and surface ships, and inflict upon them such losses that " the game will not be worth the candle." Two wars have shown how gravely this country's fighting powers can be imperilled by attacks on its life-lines—as our shipping lanes are aptly called—and in any future war these will undoubtedly be attacked with all the weight and vigour which the enemy can bring to bear against them.

Another task that falls to Coastal Command is photographic reconnaissance. In World War II hundreds of thousands of photographs of enemy and enemy-occupied territory were taken by Coastal Command, often without the enemy's knowledge. Wonderful camera lenses enabled pilots to fly at 40,000 ft. or more and to take pictures on which details of the scene below stood out as sharply as on a seaside snapshot. Highly trained officers (men and women), using special apparatus, studied these photographs and interpreted the story they had to tell. And very interesting the stories often were. They revealed the damage done by Bomber Command raids, the number of aeroplanes on an airfield, the " secret " entrances to underground factories, new buildings, the whereabouts of lurking warships and, on more than one occasion, they told us about new types of warplanes the enemy were about to bring into service. Photographic reconnaissance is the best and most reliable source of " intelligence " in spite of the many tricks which are practised to deceive the cameras and the photographic interpreters, and it enables those directing operations to work with knowledge which, but for photographic reconnaissance, they would lack.

To another branch of the R.A.F., the Tactical Air Command (now merged with an overseas command), fell work similar in prin-

[Crown Copyright Reserved.

A LECTURE ON NAVIGATION AT AN INITIAL TRAINING WING.

ciple to that of the very earliest R.F.C. squadrons which were trained to work with the Army. Its job was to give direct support to the men fighting on the ground, not only by keeping the enemy air force at bay, and stopping it from taking photographs of troop movements and dispositions on our side, and striking at them, but also by attacking tanks and all other forms of armoured vehicles, lorries, wireless stations, supply trains and even the guns of the artillery. Its aeroplanes were made up of fighters and light bombers, photographic aeroplanes, rocket-fighters and fighter-bombers. If war broke out, the Tactical Air Command would doubtless be re-formed.

THE R.A.F. IN WAR AND PEACE

Working with it, and sometimes under its fighters' protection, would be the Army's own " artillery observation post " aircraft— those little, single-engined, unarmed aeroplanes whose pilots brave rifle and machine-gun fire in their determination to find out what is going on below and to radio reports back to base from their high but dangerous grandstand. These aeroplanes are flown by Army pilots, although they are usually looked after by R.A.F. mechanics.

Last of the " operational " commands is Transport Command,

LOADING A LONG-FOCUS AIR-SURVEY CAMERA INTO AN R.A.F. ANSON.

which has the duty of transporting men and materials of the R.A.F. and the R.A.F. Regiment, and of towing the gliders of the Airborne Forces, and carrying the men of the Parachute Regiment. Transport Command also flies important officers on official journeys. It is equipped with several different types of aeroplane, ranging in size from little six-seaters to big four-engined transports capable of carrying forty or more fully equipped soldiers and all their gear.

Success in war often depends upon team work, and although each of the five operational commands has its clearly defined jobs to do, all are flexible enough to give one another a hand if circumstances should distribute the load unevenly and impose upon one

["*Flight*" *Photo.*

A FORMATION OF DELTA-WING AIRCRAFT WITH AVRO VULCAN BOMBER
AHEAD AND ASTERN.

The small deltas are Avro 707's.

more than a fair share of the burden. This is but one example of the flexibility of air power. From earliest times aeroplanes or branches of the Air Force have been able to do jobs they were not intended to do—and have been able to do them with great skill. Nevertheless, there have been occasions, fortunately few, when the weapons employed have not been equal to the task attempted.

The Royal Air Force also works in the closest harmony with the other Services. Indeed, the Army, the Royal Navy and the Royal Air Force, although each has its own duties and responsibilities, must sink their several identities and form units of a single fighting Service whose sole aim and purpose is the enemy's defeat and final overthrow. In peace-time, colleges, schools, exercises and manœuvres give full scope for all three to get to know one another, and to learn something about the problems which each faces and how they are solved.

These imitation " wars " make life in the Services more interesting, and re-kindle that spirit of competition—not only between each Service but between individual units of each Service—which builds up a good morale and makes a man take still greater pride in his work and in his unit. It does away with monotony and the feeling that even the best work serves no useful end. The fighting Services have always to be on the alert and ready for action. Wars can break out with startling suddenness ; a little exercise, a mock battle now and again, is a wonderful stimulant to enthusiasm, and the R.A.F., no less than the Army and the Navy, look forward to their annual exercises with lively interest and the keenest anticipation.

THE NON-OPERATIONAL COMMANDS

Behind the operational commands, and supporting them, are three non-operational commands (Flying Training, Technical Training and Maintenance) and Home Command. Their titles explain their roles. Flying Training Command is responsible for the efficiency of all pilots, navigators, signallers, flight engineers, and gunners before they go to the operational squadrons. It runs the schools, and supervises every stage of a pupil's development from raw material to qualified aircrew.

Technical Training Command sees that the squadrons have the best mechanics to look after their warplanes and keep them in perfect

[*Photographic News Agencies, Ltd.*

Four billowing canopies catch the sunlight as they open and check the fall of an army vehicle which has been dropped from an R.A.F. transport.

flying and operational trim. Maintenance Command supplies the squadrons with all the aeroplanes they need, with spares (such as instruments and accessories) and all the hundreds of little items needed for their efficient servicing. Maintenance Command also takes charge of aeroplanes which are too badly damaged for repair at the squadron, and if they are beyond repair removes all the serviceable instruments and accessories, checks them and if necessary puts them right, then stores them. What is left is " scrapped."

Home Command, formed in 1946 as Reserve Command, administers and controls the Royal Auxiliary Air Force, the general reserve, the Royal Air Force Volunteer Reserve, University Air Squadrons and the Air Training Corps. The functions of these different reserve forces have been described earlier. They form, as it were, a shadow Air Force which, on the outbreak of war, takes substantial form and throws its weight in with the regular Air Force.

[*Central Press*

PARATROOPERS IN AN R.A.F. TRANSPORT READY TO MAKE THEIR JUMP.

All these commands have their headquarters in the United Kingdom. There are other units overseas which come under other commands: the British Air Forces of Occupation in Germany, the Middle East Command, and the Far East Air Force. In area, the Middle East Command is probably the biggest of all commands; it embraces Malta, East Africa, Iraq, the Sudan, Cyprus and Aden, as well as the Canal Zone of Egypt. The Far East Air Force includes units at Singapore, Negombo (Ceylon), Malaya and Hong Kong.

Commands at home and overseas are so organized

[*Crown Copyright Reserved.*

P.T. INSTRUCTORS REHEARSE EXERCISES FOR DEMONSTRATION.

that they can, if necessary, work on their own for a time, but normally they receive orders direct from the Air Ministry. The Air Ministry is divided up into a great many branches, each concerned with one particular kind of work or duty. The heads of the more important branches are members of the Air Council, which runs the Air Force as a board of directors runs a business. The Air Council decides all the big matters that need careful thought and mature consideration—such as the manner in which the Air Force shall be used to achieve a certain purpose; what kind of aeroplanes shall be ordered, and how many; how large the Air Force must be to maintain its efficiency and meet its responsibilities; where new airfields shall be built, and how much shall be spent on them; what airfields shall be given up, and where new squadrons shall be formed; what old squadrons shall be disbanded. It is presided over by the Secretary of State for Air; the Vice-President is the Parliamentary Under-Secretary of State for Air, and another member is always the Chief of Air Staff.

[Fox Photos.

DOUBLY SYMBOLIC.

The Eagle with outstretched wings surmounts the R.A.F.'s War Memorial on the Victoria Embankment, London. The Superfortresses sailing overhead in a fly-past to commemorate the anniversary of the " Battle of Britain " remind us of the part played by the United States Air Force during those momentous years of World War II.

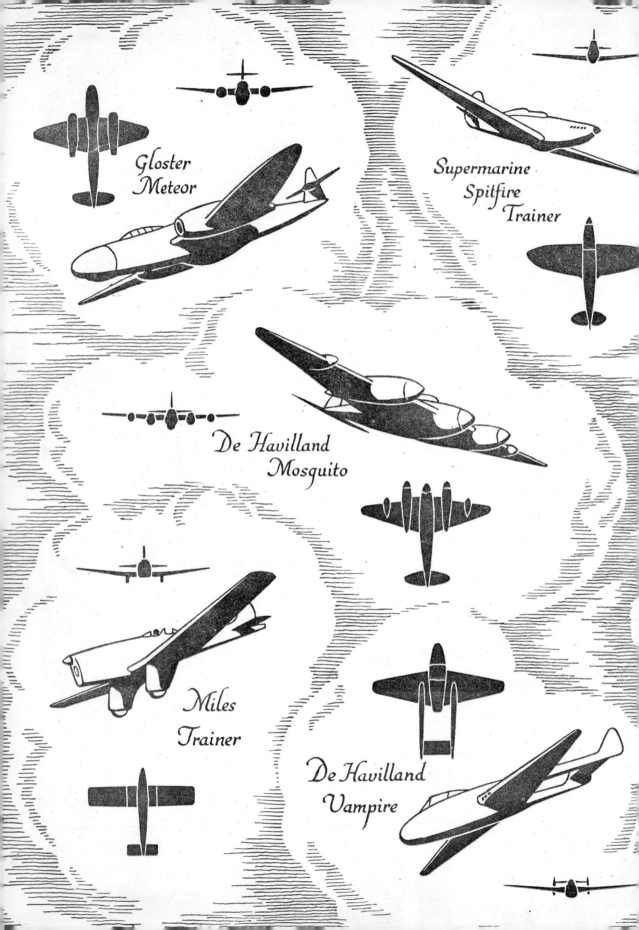

Gloster
Meteor

Supermarine
Spitfire
Trainer

De Havilland
Mosquito

Miles
Trainer

De Havilland
Vampire